THE COMPLEXITIES OF HUMAN TRAFFICKING AND EXPLOITATION

The Circles of Analysis

Craig Barlow

T0385779

P

First published in Great Britain in 2025 by

Policy Press, an imprint of
Bristol University Press
University of Bristol
1–9 Old Park Hill
Bristol
BS2 8BB
UK
t: +44 (0)117 374 6645
e: bup-info@bristol.ac.uk

Details of international sales and distribution partners are available at
policy.bristoluniversitypress.co.uk

British Library Cataloguing in Publication Data
A catalogue record for this book is available from the British Library

ISBN 978-1-4473-7246-2 paperback
ISBN 978-1-4473-7247-9 ePub
ISBN 978-1-4473-7248-6 ePdf

Cover design: Liam Roberts Design
Front cover image: Stocksy/Alicia Bock
Bristol University Press and Policy Press use environmentally
responsible print partners.
Printed and bound in Great Britain by CPI Group (UK) Ltd,
Croydon, CR0 4YY

FSC
www.fsc.org
MIX
Paper | Supporting
responsible forestry
FSC® C013604

Contents

List of figures and tables

Figures

Tables

Acknowledgements

Writing this book has been made so much easier and even more rewarding because of the encouragement and support of my family, colleagues and friends.

I wish to acknowledge the love and support of my wife, Sue and our sons, Joe and Peter, who never flinched as I embarked upon study and a research career in addition to my work as an independent practitioner.

The Circles of Analysis model began as a PhD thesis that, fittingly for a complexity-based theory, has continued to evolve and adapt, extending its applications, and testing and refining the concepts. I could not have done this without my colleagues Professor Simon Green and Dr Alicia Heys at the Wilberforce Institute, University of Hull. My thanks to them for all the 'big thoughts' sessions as we worked to develop the concept of the 'conducive environment' and figure out the mechanisms that create the opportunities for patterns of exploitation to emerge and be sustained. Their contribution cannot be underestimated.

I have received so much encouragement from academic colleagues in writing this book, in particular Professor Carole Murphy, Director of the Bakhita Centre for Research on Modern Slavery, Exploitation and Abuse at St Mary's University, Twickenham and Professor Simon Harding.

I have also had just as much interest and support from professional colleagues. Caroline Haughey KC OBE recognised the potential applications of my research in the investigation and prosecution of modern slavery cases, and former Police Superintendent Phil Brewer has assisted my research since long before his retirement and has continued to work with me ever since. Mr Kevin Hyland was the first Independent Anti-Slavery Commissioner for the UK and contributed to the earliest stages of the research that would become the Circles of Analysis, and he introduced me to so many incredible colleagues across Europe, such as lawyer Alexandra Malangone, who I thank for her advice and information and her help in producing some of the case studies in this book. Thanks also to Kevin's successor, Dame Sara Thornton, for all her support, especially when things got tough, and I needed a little courage to keep going.

Finally, thank you to my publishers, Bristol University Press, for their tireless enthusiasm, guidance and support – I could not have had a better experience in publishing my first book.

1

Introduction

In April 2015, the UK Government's much-anticipated Modern Slavery Act received Royal Assent. This, and the appointment of the first ever Anti-Slavery Commissioner, had been key components of the Modern Slavery Strategy (HM Government, 2014) which was subsequently reviewed 12 months after its implementation (Haughey, 2016b). The purpose of the review was to evaluate whether the Act was achieving its objectives. It also examined the extent to which it was assisting investigators and prosecutors in combating modern slavery in the UK context and, to a lesser extent, abroad. It represents the evolution of understanding, responses and current practices by all UK agencies to the problem. It also identified limitations, uncertainties and constraints on investigators and the need for further development of responses and statutory systems. Subsequent reviews such as the Independent Parliamentary Review of 2019 (Field, Butler-Sloss, and Miller, 2019) and evidence of Professor Dame Sara Thornton who was the former Independent Anti-Slavery Commissioner, Baroness Butler Sloss (2023), Dr Caroline Haughey OBE, KC (5 July 2023) and others to the UK House of Commons Home Affairs Committee on Human Trafficking (2023) suggest that there has been very little development of responses to the problem of modern slavery and the UK's statutory systems. If anything, it is suggested, there has been a regression. It is not only the UK that seems to be retreating from the fight against human trafficking. The latest biannual global report on Trafficking in Persons by the United Nations Office on Drugs and Crime (UNODC) indicated that there is a worldwide decrease in the number of victim identifications and convictions of traffickers and the EU's 2022 'Report on the progress made in the fight against trafficking in human beings' also noted a significant reduction in identification of victims and the number of prosecutions (European Commission, 2022, p 9).

Despite this, around the world law enforcement agencies, health agencies and protective services, lawyers, third-sector organisations and academics strive to combat human trafficking, to understand its aetiology and processes, protect and support victims, identify, disrupt and prosecute perpetrators. It's been my pleasure and privilege to work with many colleagues from diverse disciplines and backgrounds at home and abroad to further this endeavour. And this book is a small contribution to that end.

I begin this book by describing a range of activities in which people have been forced to work, provide services or engage in criminal activities by individual adults, organised crime groups (OCGs) or youth gangs. I describe the nature and extent of human trafficking and modern slavery worldwide before focusing on the nature and the present scope and scale of the phenomenon through case studies drawn from my own work as a practitioner and that of close colleagues. The names of victims and some of the traffickers and locations of the exploitation have been changed to protect the privacy of survivors. The details of the trafficking and exploitation processes are accurate accounts based upon public records and interviews with professionals. I argue that there are similarities in the characteristics of victims that are targeted for exploitation and that there are similarities in patterns of trafficking and exploitation when the experiences of those that traffic or have been trafficked and exploited are compared to others in different regions and contexts. Extreme poverty, adverse family contexts, poor education or special educational needs and disengagement from education, loss of employment, drug or substance abuse, exposure to domestic violence and prior victimisation and abandonment emerge as consistent themes in the adverse life experiences of victims prior to trafficking and exploitation, regardless of ethnic background, country or region of origin. This raises the question, however, why is it that not all people or groups with these characteristics are exploited even though some are? I question the received wisdom that these characteristics are risk factors or predictors for trafficking victimisation and argue that it is the differences between cases of trafficking and modern slavery that help us to understand how it emerges and is maintained. These differences are represented by the relationship between the victim, the exploiters and the environment in which they both exist. It is my assertion throughout this book that human trafficking, modern slavery and other forms of exploitation are more easily understood as a pattern emerging from processes of abuse, and by framing it as such, it is possible to apply theories of interpersonal violence to identify the criminogenic motivations of traffickers and exploiters in different contexts.

Responses to the problem often fail to identify a potential victim. This is due to a response that is based upon flawed assumptions about those that have been exploited, about the perpetrators and about the processes of the exploitation. Consequently, current understanding of the problem is reductive, and interventions are limited. 'Understanding human trafficking and modern slavery is not simply about identifying the characteristics of people who are vulnerable to abuse; it requires a wider perspective and understanding of the contexts, situations and relationships in which exploitation is likely to manifest' (adapted from Ofsted, 2018). This book provides that perspective by constructing the 'Circles of Analysis', a theoretical framework that explains and describes the nature and aetiology of human trafficking and modern slavery which also applies to other types of exploitation.

Background to this book

In 2010 Operation GOLF, consisting of a joint investigation team (JIT) formed between the Metropolitan Police and the Romanian National Police, tackled a specific Romanian organised crime network (OCN) that was trafficking and exploiting children from the Roma community. The investigation led to the arrest of 126 individuals. The offences included: trafficking human beings (including internal trafficking in the UK), money laundering, benefit fraud, child neglect, perverting the course of justice, theft and handling of stolen goods (Europol, 2019). In 2013 the charity Anti Trafficking and 'Race in Europe' project (Response

Against Criminal Exploitation) published research on the problem criminal exploitation of children in the UK and included reports of trafficked children forced to undertake a range of criminal activities, including ATM theft, pickpocketing, bag-snatching, counterfeit DVD selling, cannabis cultivation and benefit fraud, as well as being forced to beg (Brotherton and Waters, 2013; Anti-Slavery International, 2014).

Until recently, there has been little attention paid to the problem of child criminal exploitation (CCE) when compared with the problem of sexual exploitation. Exploitation through forced criminality has involved children and vulnerable adults from within the UK as well as those trafficked into the UK and trafficking for multiple purposes seems to be an increasing trend; for example, early and forced marriage is often a conduit to sexual exploitation, forced labour and domestic servitude.

The need for theory-informed approaches

I have come to writing this book following 30 years' practice as a forensic social worker and specialist in safeguarding children and vulnerable people. I have worked as a consultant practitioner and expert witness in both the civil and criminal justice systems, including the prosecution of complex cases of human trafficking and modern slavery. As a practitioner I have worked with both victims and perpetrators of sexual violence, physical and psychological violence, emotional abuse, neglect and exploitation in a wide variety of contexts. From this perspective I have become familiar with the challenges and complexities of trafficking and exploitation cases, the difficulties faced by other professionals from different disciplines in this field and the paucity of information and theory available to guide practice.

As a secret or hidden phenomenon, human trafficking and modern slavery is surrounded by myths, assumptions and false perceptions. These are reinforced by political agendas, sensationalist reporting and representations of victims and those engaged in intervening to stop the trade or to 'rescue' the victims. In Chapter 4, I will demonstrate and discuss how all these elements coalesce to form complex systems in which abuse and exploitation are maintained. The abuse and exploitation adapt to new pressures and opportunities but at the same time maintain their cohesion, based upon the congruent characteristics of suitable targets for exploitation, the needs and motivations of both those that are exploited and those that exploit, and the context in which the exploitation occurs.

There is an absence of a coherent, aetiological model that describes and explains human trafficking and modern slavery. So far, the research in the field of human trafficking has been dominated by sexual exploitation and this research itself has focused upon female victims primarily so that the sexual exploitation of young males has been largely overlooked (Nicholls et al, 2014). Existing guidance for safeguarding practitioners, law enforcement officers and lawyers has been dominated by checklists of signs and indicators of human trafficking and linear processes of intervention represented by simplistic flow charts and of so-called indicators and 'risk factors'. Consequently, efforts to define and describe what constitutes human trafficking and modern slavery, servitude, forced and compulsory labour, sexual and criminal exploitation and so forth, are inadequate due to their rigidity and inability to adapt to such a dynamic and evolutionary phenomenon. The evolution of definitions and concepts of trafficking, slavery and abuse are presented in Chapters 2 and 3 and the current challenges and frustrations faced by professionals in this field are presented in these chapters. This book therefore eschews existing linear approaches to develop a theory of human trafficking and modern slavery that explains and describes the problem relationally, as a pattern that emerges from the interaction of people within complex systems over time. In so doing it resolves many of the current difficulties faced by practitioners who must assess risk to children, families, vulnerable adults and communities, investigate crime, prosecute offenders and safeguard people who are either being exploited, have been exploited in the past or are at risk of being exploited in the future.

The difficulties in responding to human trafficking and modern slavery

It is often difficult to identify victims of trafficking (UK Serious Organised Crime (SOC) Strategic Analysis Team, 2014; Haughey,

2016). Cases of criminal and sexual exploitation or exploitation through forced begging, shoplifting and other forms of acquisitive crime, door-to-door sales and sales of counterfeit goods are often viewed simplistically as public order issues or petty crime in which the victim is the perceived offender (UK Serious Organised Crime (SOC) Strategic Analysis Team, 2014). In this book I demonstrate that the complexity of such cases is far greater than it may appear initially. I argue therefore that investigators, probation services, safeguarding social workers, immigration and border agencies and lawyers (in both the civil and criminal justice systems) must develop a more analytical approach to assessment that includes a potential victim's relationships, experiences, behaviour and environment over time. This requires a theoretical model to assist and support professional judgement and decision-making.

Safeguarding systems and the criminal justice system require the identification of abuse or a crime through a disclosure or complaint. Trafficked and exploited people do not always self-identify for a variety of reasons that will be explored, described and explained in this book. Among those that avoid disclosing abuse and exploitation, many do not recognise that they are victims of exploitation in the first place and may not be able to do so until they are out of the exploitative relationship and environment. Evidence of exploitation must therefore be gathered by other means.

Keeping exploited people safe

It has been widely noted that children going missing from care is a major problem for safeguarding agencies and increases a child's vulnerability to predatory criminals. Anti-Slavery International suggest that a significant number of the children that go missing from care have previously been trafficked for criminal exploitation, particularly Vietnamese children. RACE in Europe found that there were 'few potential child victims of trafficking in local authority care' (Brotherton and Waters, 2013) and yet not being identified as a potential victim of trafficking is a key risk to a child going missing from care (Shipton, Setter, and Holmes, 2016).

Focusing on children and young people who had been trafficked, Shipton et al (2016) reported that groups of young survivors explained how a child might go missing to escape the demands of traffickers, implying that they did not feel that authorities could safeguard them effectively in their placement. The same research raised concerns in relation to child criminal exploitation where the children's criminality was prioritised over their vulnerability, both in terms of preventing episodes of going missing and also after the child had gone missing and during the resulting investigation.

Some victims may feel a stronger affiliation to their exploiters and traffickers than to their own families and child protection agencies. In yet other cases the exploiters may also be family members and the criminality has been justified and normalised within the victim's lived experience. The process of 'target hardening' as a means of protecting those at risk from exploitation and away from anti-social peers and predatory adults tends to be reactive and fails to take account of the complex relationship between the exploited victim and their exploiters and the dynamics of the exploitation.

Problems with definition of trafficking, modern slavery and exploitation

Difficulty in identifying people as being trafficked and exploited is partly attributable to the lack of an agreed definition of the terms and strategic guidance. While the professional discourse about trafficking and modern slavery in general acknowledges that victims often remain in contact with their exploiters even after removal from the exploitative situation, there are no commonly agreed safety and protection standards for the placement of children that are known to have been or are suspected to have been trafficked and exploited through criminal activities or provisions for safe accommodation and support for adults who have been similarly victimised. I attribute this to a lack of theoretical foundation underpinning professional and statutory responses.

The problems of definition are manifold regarding who is a victim, what constitutes exploitation and how to define traffickers and exploiters, a gang or what constitutes organised crime. Statutory definitions and duties vary between states in terms of criminal responsibility, crimes against children and women, safeguarding, application of legal instruments, responsibility and consent.

There is no consensus on definitions of what constitutes a gang, a gang member or gang activity (Decker and Kempf-Leonard, 1991; Bjerregaard, 2002). The term 'street gang' tends to be used to describe any group of young people from those who spend their leisure time on the streets together to those engaged in serious and coordinated criminality.

What constitutes organised crime is similarly contentious: some scholars define organised crime in terms of criminal structures, others in terms of activities. Klaus von Lampe, for instance, has collated some 200 definitions of organised crime (von Lampe, 2019). While some aspects of CCE, for instance, link directly to organised crime such as running drugs, money and weapons for drug dealers, others do not.

Criminalisation of victims

Shipton et al (2016) found that being criminalised (for example, being arrested or prosecuted) seems to make trafficked people more likely to go missing. Their survey of trafficked children found that 65 per cent of respondents from the not-for-profit sector and 38 per cent from the criminal justice sector agreed that criminalisation has an impact on children, increasing the likelihood of them absconding from care.[1]

Although non-prosecution principles exist in EU law and policy,[2] there is no shared international consensus on a framework or standards for non-criminalisation to which legislators might be

---

[1] 'Heading back to harm: a study of trafficked and unaccompanied children going missing from care in the UK'. This research attempted to quantify the number of unaccompanied asylum-seeking children and children who may be trafficked in the UK care system, as well as the number who go missing from care.

[2] The principle of non-punishment of *the victim for crimes they have been involved in as a consequence of their trafficking*. Article 26 of the Council of Europe Convention on Action Against Trafficking of Human Beings states: 'Each Party shall, in accordance with the basic principles of its legal system, provide for the possibility of not imposing penalties on victims for their involvement in unlawful activities, to the extent that they have been compelled to do so' (Council of Europe, 2005).

required to adhere. Consequently, criminal justice responses and processes are inconsistent across regions (Barlow, 2022) and victims of criminal exploitation continue to be prosecuted for crimes that they have been forced to commit. Bijan Hoshi (2013) attributes this to the vision of non-criminalisation being inadequate at both regional (which is to say European) level and the local level of individual jurisdictions such as the UK.

In England and Wales, for instance, the non-punishment principle was made a provision the Modern Slavery Act 2015 with the inclusion of the statutory defence under section 45. However, this has been the subject of extensive legal debate over the application of the defence, thresholds and relevance of evidence, who may or may not be considered an actual or potential victim of trafficking within the scope of the defence.[3] These are, of course, technical arguments on interpretation of points of law but nevertheless have a considerable impact on policy development and frontline practice in the field of investigation, safeguarding of victims, prosecutions of perpetrators and support and compensation for survivors (Barlow, 2022; Heys et al, 2022). The problem caused by developing policy based upon legal interpretations is a pervasive lack of understanding of the normative and conceptual grounding of human trafficking and modern slavery (Jovanovic, 2017), and a general failure to grasp the subtle and nefarious methods by which traffickers can exert total dominance over trafficked persons (Hoshi, 2013).

Criminal justice responses

Current responses to the problem of trafficking and modern slavery are predicated upon identification of victims and their traffickers and exploiters, investigation of abuse through exploitation and trafficking and prosecution of perpetrators, thus are rooted in criminal justice approaches to the abuse and exploitation of vulnerable people (Moore, 1995; Gadd and Broad, 2018; Barlow, 2022). The criminal justice approach emphasises the identification

---

[3]   See for example: *DPP v M* [2020] EWHC 344 Admin; [2021] 1 WLR 1669; *R v Brecanni* [2021] EWCA Crim 731; *R v AAD, AAH and AAI* [2022] EWCA Crim 106 and *VCL v United Kingdom* 77587/12 (16 February 2021).

of a crime, views the motivations of the criminal as an important cause of the crime and responds to this through the imposition of sanctions. As such it is a largely reactive approach. The person who is suspected of committing the crime is the person who has been caught engaging in the criminal act. This creates a dilemma: how to respond proportionately to a person who is both an offender, and a victim whose offending is a consequence of their victimisation. There is therefore a tension between the goals of the criminal justice system and those of the safeguarding system.

Social care responses

Safeguarding models in health and social care tend to situate the problem with the victim and their family (Firmin et al, 2016). They adopt an alternative approach that emphasises prevention of abuse and exploitation through the identification and reduction of 'risk factors' such as vulnerability and adversity. This is a target-hardening approach that emphasises building a protective environment and strengthening resilience.

Traditionally statutory safeguarding systems have focused upon younger children and the risk of intra-familial abuse and neglect. More recently, the contextual safeguarding approach in the UK (Firmin, 2017) has been achieving traction at the policy level. This approach combines open systems theory and principles of situational crime prevention and routine activities, in order to understand a child's vulnerability and resilience, exposure to threats and sources of protection in their social contexts beyond family and home. This approach is helping to address the needs of older children who are outside of the home for far greater periods of time and exposed to different risks compared with younger children (Longfield, 2019).

Critique of current responses

The Criminal Justice System and the Health and Social Care System share a common concern over abuse through trafficking and exploitation, but they perceive the results differently: the Criminal Justice System identifies a criminal event; the safeguarding community identifies harm to a victim (adapted from Moore, 1995). Between the two approaches is a gulf of concepts, principles, practice and values. Both can be equally reductive in terms of their explanation of causes of trafficking and exploitation of human beings. However, attempts to respond to human trafficking and various forms of modern slavery and exploitation reflect the dominance of the criminal justice approach in both policy (HM Government, 2015) and practice, which emphasises the need to respond to the problem as a crime first and a safeguarding issue second. For instance, a person may be arrested for committing a street crime such as shoplifting, ATM theft, pickpocketing, bag theft or even burglary. If they are below the age of criminal responsibility they will not be prosecuted. If the property is recovered the crime may be recorded as detected and cleared up and the child released with no further action, potentially back to their exploiters (Love, 2017). Some exploiters of children have deliberately targeted children under the age of 10 years because they will not be prosecuted (Haughey, 2016a). Among older children, those who have been found to be criminally exploited have often been arrested and prosecuted two or three times previously before being recognised as victims of exploitation (Southwell, 2018). Clearly the goals of the two systems are contiguous and therefore have the potential to be far more effective through integrated, collaborative approaches to the problem.

Since 2017, the contextual safeguarding approach has offered much, not only in developing greater collaboration not only between police and social services, but also developing engagement between statutory services and community groups, local businesses and the general public. Gradually, new local safeguarding arrangements have begun to emerge (such as those in Lincolnshire, Newham East Riding and others), with a focus on contextual safeguarding, and such arrangements have been found to have the potential to make this level of integration happen (Longfield, 2019). While the contextual safeguarding approach sets out how and why such integration should be achieved, it does not offer a theory for child trafficking and exploitation. A truly integrated response from frontline professionals requires investigators, assessors and decision-makers to be able to identify, understand the phenomenon of human trafficking and exploitation and be able to communicate using shared knowledge and specialist insights within a mutually helpful organising framework. There is currently no such framework available due to the lack of research and theory development in the field of trafficking and modern slavery. This book, therefore, seeks to advance the achievements of the contextual safeguarding approach to develop practice in the contexts of social work risk assessment and management, criminal investigation and legal proceedings, and apply these ideas to the trafficking and exploitation of adults as well as children.

The neglect of the issue in the research literature may be due to such crimes inevitably involving hidden or hard to reach communities. It has been extremely difficult for researchers to obtain sample groups that are representative of trafficked and exploited people as a whole (Tyldum and Brunovskis, 2005). Much of the existing research has focused primarily on sexual exploitation of women and girls and, more recently, labour exploitation (Chuang, 2014). Nevertheless, the body of empirical data relating to human trafficking and modern slavery abuses is growing. In 2017, the UK Home Secretary, Amber Rudd, said that although a large body of data exists, modern slavery is still largely not understood; she suggested that some even doubt that it really exists (Rudd, 2017). I argue that the lack of understanding to which the Home Secretary referred is due to the lack of a theoretical framework with which to organise and interpret the mass of data that has been so far collated. The consequence of this is that practice in working to prevent such abuse, safeguard exploited children from re-victimisation and identify and prosecute offenders is undermined.

Proper identification of trafficking and modern slavery can only occur if we are sensitised to look for something and recognise it as worthy of investigation. Investigation involves the seeking, finding and interpreting of evidence that leads towards (or away) from a hypothesis for what has happened. The interpretation of the evidence is dependent upon theory. If modern slavery is only conceptualised in terms of crime and perpetrator first and foremost, with a secondary concern for the victim impact, we distort and bias our understanding of the event and limit the range of responses (Perrow, 1999). Similarly, if we only conceptualise the problem in terms of the vulnerability of the victim and the harm that has been, or is likely to be, suffered, we fail to understand the victim's relationship with the perpetrators of the abuse and the processes involved. A theory is explanatory: it therefore enables us to develop a narrative to describe events and experiences, by informing the relevant questions that drive the inquiry, organise evidence and make pragmatic, informed decisions and plans.

The current state of knowledge is uneven. This reflects the fact that organisations, researchers and practitioners inevitably seek out and analyse data relevant to their specialist areas and interests influenced by their needs and objectives but is only an overview of such research that reveals some consistencies. To overcome this problem, this thesis synthesises the most helpful elements from diverse and sometimes conflicting theories with my own thoughts and ideas to construct a new theory: the 'Circles of Analysis'.

Purpose of this book

This book conceptualises the problem of human trafficking and modern slavery *relationally*: it will enable the reader to interpret the activities and processes of trafficking and modern slavery, and other forms of exploitation and abuse in terms of the context of relationships between the child, the perpetrator and the environment from which they both emerge and in which they both exist.

It has always been my intention to produce research that would have practical value to investigators, prosecutors and practitioners engaged in safeguarding people at risk of trafficking, as well as those who are being subjected to or have been subjected to different forms of exploitation and abuse in the past. This intention was clearly informed by underlying concepts of human rights to social justice, well-being and safety. The research must be academically viable, valid and robust, but it needs to be comprehensible also to people outside of both my professional and academic disciplines (Coomans, Grünfeld, and Kamminga, 2010), and it needs to have utility for those that may wish to use the findings both in the UK and beyond (Lynham, 2002; Hart et al, 2003). This has been a guiding principle in the development and evaluation of the Circles of Analysis model.

To this end, the book will answer the following questions:

(1) What are the components and mechanisms that maintain the relationships between the victim, their environment and the perpetrators that lead to human trafficking and modern slavery?

(2) Precisely how can the relational understanding of trafficking and exploitation have proposed in this book result in better strategic and tactical responses by organisations concerned with safeguarding victims, and pursuing and prosecuting traffickers and perpetrators of modern slavery and exploitation?

(3) How can a theoretical model for understanding of trafficking and modern slavery be applied across different professional disciplines and different exploitation contexts?

Structure of this book

I begin by describing the nature and processes of human trafficking and the debates and controversies concerning definitions and terminology such as modern slavery and the nature of exploitation. I argue the case for understanding human trafficking and modern slavery as a process of interactions between victims, perpetrators and others in their environments that produces patterns of exploitation. I argue that while most often the main motivation for human trafficking, modern slavery and other forms of exploitation is profit and gain, the sadistic nature and degrees of violence visited upon the exploited people is gratuitous; it is excessive in terms of the force that would be sufficient to achieve that gain. Understanding motivation for different types of exploitation of people, including children, in terms of material profit and gain only does not account for this violent victimisation as a major characteristic of the phenomenon. To address this, I proceed to draw upon and integrate the professional and academic knowledge relating to criminogenic drivers of violence.

To investigate the underlying knowledge or assumptions that inform current responses by statutory and non-governmental organisations (NGOs) to human trafficking, modern slavery and exploitation, I will present an overview of current policy and practice: Chapter 2 investigates the evolution of the current terminology and legislation and its influence on policy and practice specifically in relation to the problem. Some of the underlying assumptions are revealed and discussed.

The principles of professional practice in relation to investigating traffickers and protecting victims is the widely adopted strategy known as the '4 Ps' paradigm: Pursue, Prevent, Prepare and Protect. I will critically examine processes for identification of those at risk, pursuit and prosecution of offenders, and the development of safeguarding strategies. I will propose a working definition of 'exploitation' developed with my colleagues Professor Simon Green and Dr Alicia Heys, providing terms of reference for the critical evaluation of criminal justice and safeguarding responses to the problem in the rest of the book.

The middle chapters of this book develop the points in the second chapter and demonstrate how a pattern of exploitation emerges from the interaction between the suitable target for exploitation, the perpetrator and the environment in which both operate over time. A case study approach will be taken, using cases in which I or close colleagues have been involved at different times. I criticise recent attempts to formulate typologies of exploitation such as the International Labour Organization's Operational Indicators of Human Trafficking, the UNODC Trafficking Indicators and the UK Home Office 'A Typology of Modern Slavery Offences in the UK' (Cooper et al, 2017) as distracting and counterproductive because such typologies tend to oversimplify a multifaceted and complex phenomenon such as human trafficking and modern slavery. While it may be argued that such types and typologies, as those developed for the UK Government Home Office, identify, order and simplify data so that they can be described in terms that are comparable (McKinney, 1969), the concentration on shared characteristics of a number of cases gives the impression of clearly identifiable and distinct categories of trafficking and modern slavery. It fails to account for the ways in which people may be exploited in multiple ways across different contexts, over time or simultaneously which may account for how few traffickers have been prosecuted. A person who is trafficked for the purposes of criminal exploitation must be sourced from somewhere; the provider of the that person may be the first party to gain from the exploitation and may be the person's own family, social network or community, corrupt officials or others in positions of authority and trust or influence. In the case of exploitation by family members, the offenders, controllers and end users may all be one and the same (as in cases of domestic servitude).

Victims of human trafficking, modern slavery and other forms of exploitation may pass through the hands of many parties before they are identified. Furthermore, a victim that is being used for criminal exploitation is immediately vulnerable to other forms of exploitation and abuse (Finkelhor, 2008). The nature of the abuse will therefore depend largely on the motivations, needs and interests of the perpetrators and the value that the victim represents to them. This can vary between perpetrators, criminals and crime groups or networks.

A person that is exploited for one form of exploitation may only be of value for a limited period of time (for example, they may become too old or too big or more conspicuous). They must then either be utilised in a different way or disposed of. When a victim is no longer able to fulfil one role they may become better suited to recruitment or maintaining discipline among other victims, or maybe move into other areas of the criminal enterprise if that fits with the needs of the crime group and profits and gains continue to be made. Disposal of the victim by the perpetrators of exploitation may involve returning them to the family or community (Shelley, 2011), trading of the victim, abandonment or murder of the victim. The disposal method gives significant insights into the nature of the crime group; that is, their business models, activities, competence and expertise, connections with other criminals and crime groups and their interface with the legitimate economy and services.

A typology such as that proposed by the UK's Home Office leads to 'top-down' linear logic ('If trafficking/slavery/servitude/forced labour, then these characteristics'). This distracts by providing an unrealistic description of the problem and is counterproductive because it limits professional enquiry and contributes to linear flow charts for decision-making and professional intervention. The 'Circles of Analysis' model proposed in this book takes a 'bottom-up' approach that enables the user to organise data in such a way as to identify patterns of interactions or relationships from which emerges exploitation as an output of a complex of interacting systems.

In the first half I therefore argue for the need to understand exploitation, first and foremost, as a pattern of abuse. In so doing, it is possible to draw upon existing knowledge and experience in professional and academic literature on violence, abuse and neglect and integrate this with clinical experience. Chapter 3 concludes by establishing the need for a sound concept of exploitation as a mode of abuse built upon a solid theoretical foundation to take account of and better utilise existing resources, measures and remedies.

From this position I proceed to the formulation of the 'Circles of Analysis' for human trafficking, modern slavery and other forms of exploitation, which informs practice and interventions by enabling practitioners to make better use of the most robust statutory frameworks for safeguarding survivors and vulnerable people. Thus Chapter 7 is the keystone of this book, synthesising complex systems theory with other theoretical principles to produce a new, explanatory theory for human trafficking and modern slavery. The first part of the chapter develops the assertion of Chapter 4, that exploitation is a pattern that emerges from a process of abuse, maltreatment and neglect, arguing that while much has been achieved in understanding such maltreatment, in the intra-familial context, significantly less attention has been paid to extra-familial abuse. I argue that to date, research has neglected motivation of perpetrators of trafficking and modern slavery and the relationship between them and the victims in the aetiology of such abuse. I draw upon the fields of developmental psychology and criminology for theories of violence against women and children, as well as other contexts for interpersonal violence and abuse. The chapter proposes the 'Circles of Analysis' as a theoretical model as a direct challenge to the dominant reductive, descriptive explanations that underpin policy and practice in the field of human trafficking and anti-slavery practices, policies and law enforcement.

Previous approaches to understanding the problem of modern slavery have been hindered by a 'segregative' approach to not only theory development (Kalmar and Sternberg, 1988) but also practice guidance and service design. I have worked to overcome this problem by developing an integrative model of human trafficking and modern slavery; a theory that 'integrates the best aspects of a set of given theories with one's own ideas regarding the domain under investigation, instead of emphasising those features that discriminate among theories to provide a unifying explanation of the problem' (Kalmar and Sternberg, 1988; Ward and Siegert, 2002).

The Circles of Analysis model was originally developed to address the problem of trafficking of children for the purposes of forced criminality (CCE). In conducting the research to develop the model I engaged with frontline practitioners from different disciplines to gain critical responses to the Circles of Analysis as a unifying, explanatory theory of CCE, thereby informing and supporting practice across disciplines. This was an innovative approach to the research and refinement of the theoretical model. Within the disciplines of criminology, in health and social work, focus groups as a research method have frequently been used to test and evaluate programmes and gain feedback and opinions from diverse professionals. Focus groups have also had wider applications in product design and testing, market research and strategic development in the fields of politics, media and business. For the purposes of this research I used the method to test the real-world applications of the model and to explore its utility for professionals who must make statutory decisions in the field of CCE.

The focus groups not only evaluated the model but also yielded valuable insights into the processes of CCE and the characteristics of exploiters and exploited children. The participants drew upon their practice experience to collaborate with me in refining and developing the model to its final iteration.

Since the completion of that first thesis (Barlow, 2019) the model has continued to be applied to different contexts and patterns of exploitation through case work, further research (Murphy et al, 2022; Green, Heys, and Barlow, forthcoming), knowledge exchange events,[4] conferences and

---

[4]   For example: 'Understanding Organized Crime in the Context of Ukrainian Conflict, War Crimes Investigations and Enhancing Multi-Agency Cooperation and Coordination', Human Rights League, Johns Hopkins University and Kids in Need of Defence (KIND), Europe, 22–24 August 2022, Košice, Slovakia; 'Hearing the Voices of Ukrainian Children and

seminars[5] (Barlow, 2023), and publications (Barlow et al, 2021; Barlow, 2022; Heys et al, 2022).

A note on the approach to this theory

As well as exploring the academic literature within the field of human trafficking and the wider field of abuse of children, women and other vulnerable groups and protection, intra-familial and extra-familial violence and exploitation, I have taken an approach that seeks testimonial evidence and analyses policy and practice as the basis for developing an explanatory model.

This book tries to eschew a needs or deficit approach that characterises trafficked people as passive victims (O'Connell Davidson, 2010; Heys, 2023; McClintock, n.d.), instead recognising trafficked people as active agents with individual stories, aspirations and resilience. I have also actively sought critical comments and advice from a range of practitioners from the fields of law enforcement, social work and family and criminal justice systems, as well as other academics.

By adopting this approach, I anticipated that I would be able to document not only characteristics of patterns of behaviour of children and adults that are targeted for exploitation, but also the perpetrators of exploitation, and the institutions and policies that facilitate abuse and exploitation. Crucially, however, I needed contributions from people that have been trafficked and from traffickers themselves.

Four central constructs of the approach to production of this theory

In a critical examination of human-rights-based approaches to research, Maschi (2016) proposes four central constructs to

---

Young People: Child Helplines Responding to the Ukrainian Crisis', Child Helpline International and UNICEF, 27–29 March 2023, Prague.

[5] For example: 'Closing the Loophole: the absence of safeguarding protocols to protect the victims of child trafficking', Slavery Past, Present and Future, 6th Global Meeting, 11–13 July 2022, Webster Leiden Campus-Webster University US, The Netherlands.

conceptualise the rights–based approach. These constructs are also relevant to this research: human rights are a necessary condition for achieving social justice and well-being of people, their families and communities. These in turn are shaped by cultural relativism (Maschi, 2016). This is particularly important: cultures differ by how they understand and how they respond to human rights in general and children's rights in particular; they also vary in terms of who is considered a victim, concepts of work and labour and what may or may not constitute exploitation and harm (Ballet et al, 2002). Cultural relativism, according to Maschi, is grounded in notions of community autonomy and self-determination, which may trump human and children's rights. When these four central constructs are applied, human trafficking, modern slavery and other forms of exploitation potentially represent a complex problem in terms of social justice, well-being potential and actual victims, well-being of families and the wider communities that share diverse cultural backgrounds and locations. Cultural relativism also challenges the universality of UN declarations and conventions because they are ideologically and culturally orientated towards Western values and norms (Ballet et al, 2002).

Consequently, I concluded that while linear models of causation and quantitative research methods have contributed to an understanding of the scale and scope of the problem of human trafficking and modern slavery, such approaches offer limited insights into the root causes and complex relational dynamics of the problem. Therefore, the research that led to this book was designed to be inductive, combining the use of written sources and case studies with qualitative participatory research techniques. These techniques were combined to construct a theoretical model and evaluate its credibility with professionals and its utility in the field.

Assumptions of this approach

In developing my approach, I have made an assumption that understanding human trafficking and modern slavery should be based explicitly upon the norms and values set out in the International Declaration of Human Rights and the United Nations Convention on the Rights of the Child (these together with other treaties, conventions, declarations and mechanisms for the protection of rights are presented and discussed in Chapter 2). On this basis, states are morally obliged to implement policies and programmes which adhere to international laws and standards: a decent standard of living, healthcare, education and protection against abuse and exploitation are all human rights (Henry-Lee, 2005), therefore a central dynamic of my approach is an effort to identify root causes of social issues, empowering 'rights holders' (that is, recognising victims of trafficking as actors within the exploitation with needs, goals and aspirations) while 'duty bearers' are enabled to meet their obligations in upholding the rights and protecting the welfare of those that might be, or have been, targeted for exploitation and trafficking.

Some problems with this approach

Coomans, Grünfeld, and Kamminga (2010) found that legal scholars and social scientists tend broadly to adopt different approaches: they describe lawyers as 'system builders who rely on logic to determine whether arguments are compatible with an existing normal framework', so that legal scholarship tends not to address legal systems 'on the ground' and the lived experience of people working within or under those systems. Consequently, even human–rights–based legal scholarship is sometimes at risk of remaining disconnected from reality. Social scientists, on the other hand, attempt to understand social phenomena. Their findings can be empirically challenged and verified but risk ignoring or misinterpreting applicable legal standards. There is also a danger of leaning towards an over-reliance on secondary sources (Coomans, Grünfeld, and Kamminga, 2010). The approach that I have adopted in this thesis is intended to integrate these approaches for their relative strengths but in doing so there is a risk that the approach could amplify the methodological problems of each.

Overcoming problems and finding opportunities

Recognising these potential difficulties requires some reflection on my own professional and academic orientation towards the subject of human trafficking. As a practitioner I worked extensively within both the public law family justice system and criminal justice system, and I held statutory duties regarding safeguarding of children and vulnerable adults. My second academic career has provided me with a solid grounding in social sciences, and criminology in particular. In many respects these dual perspectives are a strength in this research, but the criticisms made by Coomans, Grünfeld and Kamminga resonated strongly. The risk of the pitfalls they describe has been ever present, so that a strategy to counter or at least minimise these potential errors was always required. I also held conversations with practitioner and academic colleagues from within my professional network, which allowed me to gain perspectives from professionals in Russia, Ukraine, Poland, Italy and Ireland. Integrating their perspectives into the data and inviting their views, advice and guidance has been vitally important in identifying and correcting my own biases. The design of the model has therefore striven to include the active participation of professionals and academics from other disciplines. This strategy has been a highly reflexive process throughout the research, beginning in the initial stages of enquiry.

It became my intention to produce a piece of research that would have practical value to investigators, prosecutors and practitioners engaged in safeguarding people at risk of trafficking and modern slavery, as well as those who are being subjected to or have been subjected to exploitation and abuse in the past. This intention was clearly informed by underlying concepts of human rights to social justice, well-being and safety. The research would need to be academically viable, valid and robust, but it needed to be comprehensible also to people outside of both my professional and academic disciplines (Coomans, Grünfeld, and Kamminga, 2010) and it needed to have utility for those that may wish to use the findings (Lynham, 2002; Hart et al, 2003).This has been a guiding principle in the development and evaluation of the Circles of Analysis model.

Mindful of Coomans, Grünfeld and Kamminga's admonishment of some social science researchers for their over-reliance upon secondary sources, I nevertheless decided to undertake a desk-based search for open-source interviews with victims and traffickers and exploiters, as well as drawing on the case examples that are documented within the public domain of which I and my close colleagues have first-hand experience. Accessing television news items and documentary programmes by reputable agencies and journalists, I was able to watch and transcribe interviews with victims and perpetrators who had been engaged in trafficking, modern slavery and various types of exploitation in different contexts, such as forced begging, drug and gang-based criminality, labour exploitation and domestic servitude.

These powerful testimonies of people from different social and cultural contexts, of both male and female gender and of different ages, illustrated the diversity of people that are recruited, but also drew attention to similarities between them, the patterns of their abuse and exploitation, and the relationship between them and their exploiters and the social contexts in which they existed. I would be later able to compare these recorded accounts with the first-hand experiences of police officers and social workers, prosecutors, defenders and civil lawyers, all of whom work directly with victims and perpetrators and, in some instances, people who have transitioned into perpetrator roles. By identifying and documenting these case studies I was able to develop the concept of the Circles of Analysis but also develop these ideas along a continuum of complexity.

Conclusion

I do not seek in this book to develop social policy regarding human trafficking and modern slavery other than to challenge the current assumptions that inform policy and strategic responses. Rather, my objective is to develop usable theory, to develop a robust framework that supports and guides professional judgement and decision-making, reliably informs practice and contributes to professional confidence in responding to a problem that is of great complexity.

To this end, as well as drawing upon extant theory I will draw upon the direct input of practitioners as 'experts by experience'. This is a boldly innovative approach but one that will, I believe, ensure that the Circles of Analysis not only reflects the reality and complexity of, but also responds to the needs of those professionals entrusted with investigating the phenomenon, assessing and managing risk to those who might be targeted for exploitation, disrupting and prosecuting exploiters and the longer-term survivors towards safety and recovery.

It is not possible to just arrest away human trafficking or create ever more intrusive and controlling measures to protect vulnerable people from exploitation. The problem is complex; it is non-linear; it is a pattern that emerges from the relationships between targeted people, motivated exploiters and the environments from which they emerge and in which they coexist over time. Therefore, this book represents a new, complex systems-based theory for the development of research and practice in the field of human trafficking and modern slavery. It provides a theoretical framework that describes and explains the complexity of relationships and processes of exploitation. It achieves this by describing the nature and extent of human trafficking at present; investigating the underlying knowledge or assumptions that inform current responses. Finally, it conceptualises the problem human trafficking, modern slavery and exploitation *relationally*: a way to interpret the activities and processes of exploitation of human beings in terms of the context of relationships between the suitable target for exploitation, the motivated perpetrator and the environment.

2

Concepts of trafficking, slavery and organised crime

Methods of coercive control of people for trafficking and exploitation through slavery, servitude, forced labour and the trade in human organs is frequently acknowledged within key strategies and policies produced by different governments and their agencies, but rarely is it described or explained in any detail. This contrasts with the attention that is given to the trafficking and abuse of primarily women and girls, in the context of sexual exploitation.

The aim of this chapter is to examine the evolution of current strategies and its influence on policy and practice specifically in relation to the problem of modern slavery and human trafficking. By so doing I will identify, then discuss, some of the underlying assumptions that have informed or contributed to the present state of policy and professional practice, the identification, pursuit and prosecution of offenders, and the development of prevention and safeguarding strategies.

When the Modern Slavery Bill was introduced, leading the way to the Modern Slavery Act 2015 in the UK, the then Home Secretary (later Prime Minister) Theresa May commended the legislation as ground-breaking and evidence of the UK leading the world in the fight against modern slavery. Some may feel that by 2023, the UK was leading the retreat from that battle. I shall begin by setting the UK's strategy and policy development in the wider context of international efforts through a broad overview of relevant conventions and protocols; these are crucial to understanding some of the key concepts that underpin local strategies and legislation.

I shall also review social research data and associated strategies and policies that contributed directly to the development of the current UK Modern Slavery Strategy and development of similar legislation elsewhere and examine practice guidance that has been influenced by it. With an overview established of the research that has led to the strategy and subsequent policies and procedural guidance established, I set out a working definition of 'exploitation'. This provides terms of reference for the critical evaluation of criminal justice and safeguarding responses to the problem.

The evolution of definitions and descriptions

The formal abolition of slavery in the 19th century was undeniably a major achievement in the face of stubborn resistance from an establishment that had become dependent upon the trade's huge economic rewards. This achievement nevertheless had important limitations in both its scope and effect that are frequently overlooked (Quirke, 2006). In some respects, the formal abolition of the transatlantic slave trade (specifically the ownership and sale of Black African slaves) has inadvertently created the opportunity for the illicit and more diverse slave market that may be referred to as modern-day or contemporary slavery. The strong abolitionist arguments of the 19th century may also influence modern popular understanding of what slavery is or may look like: slavery has changed and adapted through time and is influenced by politics; cultural, social, moral or religious values; and migration, war, colonialism, natural disaster and social and global economics. An understanding of the dynamics of modern slavery as an activity or process cannot be achieved without taking into account these contexts.

The word 'slavery' today incorporates more than the traditional chattel slavery and medieval serfdom: it covers a variety of abuses of human rights. This diversity of activity has made definitions of the problem and identification of its existence and scale difficult (Quirke, 2006). In 1991, the UN High Commissioner for Human Rights published a factsheet that included 'slavery-like practices' specific to the exploitation of children that included the sale of children, child prostitution, child pornography, the exploitation of child labour, the sexual mutilation of female children, the use of children in armed conflicts and debt bondage (UN Office of the High Commissioner for Human Rights – OHCHR, 1991). This list demonstrated how the range of abusive and exploitative activities that are recognised as 'slavery-like practices' has continued to grow; however, the UN High Commissioner's list did not include domestic servitude and nor did it include the coercion and control of children and vulnerable adults to engage in criminal activity, perhaps demonstrating the evolutionary nature of our understanding and growing intolerance to such practices in society.

Quirke points out that the nature and forms of abuse are not discrete from each other, often coexisting and overlapping in terms of the nature of the abuse, targets of the abuse and objectives of the abusers, who are always adaptable and open to new exploitative opportunities. This leads to substantial difficulties in formulating a coherent rationale which links offenders, victims and exploitative criminal practices together (Quirke, 2006).

These difficulties have led to not only extensive academic debate, but also political debate and effort, in order to produce a range of protocols, treaties and instruments for the detection and control of trafficking of human beings and slavery or slavery-like practices. While various definitions and instruments have been accepted or rejected in different jurisdictions, it is necessary to identify the most important in terms of their relevance to the development of national strategies, legislation and policies regarding trafficking and different types and contexts for exploitation of human beings.

The 'Slavery, Servitude, Forced Labour and Similar Institutions and Practices Convention 1926', known as the '1926 Slavery Convention' was established under the auspices of the League of Nations. The Convention provided the foundation for the prevention and suppression of the slave trade across the world and in colonial jurisdictions[1] establishing rules and articles by which slavery and the trade in slaves were banned.

---

[1]   The Abolition of Slavery Act 1833 abolished slavery in *most* of the British Empire with the exception of 'the Territories in the Possession of the East India Company', the 'Island of Ceylon' and 'the Island of Saint Helena'.

The Convention defined slavery as 'the status or condition of a person over whom any or all of the powers attaching to the right of ownership are exercised' (United Nations). This definition went through further refinements in the UN Convention on Human Rights Supplementary Convention (United Nations, 1956) but, prior to these developments, the International Labour Organization made considerable progress on the issue of forced and compulsory labour with the Forced Labour Convention, 1930. This convention sought to build upon the 1926 Slavery Convention (which undertook to 'suppress the use of forced or compulsory labour in all its forms') and defined forced or compulsory labour thus: 'For the purposes of this Convention the term forced or compulsory labour shall mean all work or service, which is exacted from any person under the menace of any penalty and for which the said person has not offered himself voluntarily' (International Labour Organization, 1930).

The Convention introduced important limitations to what constituted forced or compulsory labour[2] but also made illegal exaction of forced or compulsory labour a criminal offence (Article 25).

Perhaps the most famous and influential development in the safeguarding of human beings against violence, oppression and exploitation was the Universal Declaration of Human Rights (UDHR) that was proclaimed by the United Nations General Assembly in 1948. It is generally accepted as a major milestone in the developmental history of human rights as it set out fundamental rights to be universally protected. The relevance

---

[2] 'Forced or Compulsory Labour does not include: (a) compulsory military service laws for work of a purely military character; (b) any part of the normal civic obligations of the citizens of a fully self-governing country; (c) any work as a consequence of a conviction in a court of law, provided that the said work or service is carried out under the supervision and control of a public authority and that the said person is not hired to or placed at the disposal of private individuals, companies or associations; (d) any work or service in cases of emergency, that is, in the event of war or of a calamity, and in general any circumstance that would endanger the existence or the well-being of the population; (e) minor communal services can therefore be considered as normal civic obligations incumbent upon the members of the community.' (Article 4, § 3, European Convention on Human Rights)

and impact of the UDHR cannot be underestimated as it has been the keystone of the international human rights movement, incorporating both the 1926 Slavery Convention and the ILO Forced and Compulsory Labour Convention to clearly state in its Article 4 that: 'No one shall be held in slavery or servitude; slavery and the slave trade shall be prohibited in all their forms.'

In 1950 the Council of Europe opened the Convention for the Protection of Human Rights and Fundamental Freedoms (better known as the European Convention for Human Rights) for signature in Rome. It came into force in 1953 and was the first instrument to give effect to certain of the rights stated in the UDHR and make them binding on signatories. It also established the European Court of Human Rights (Council of Europe, n.d.).

Article 4 of the Council of Europe Human Rights Convention is born of the 1948 Declaration of Human Rights, adopting the same Article 4 statement on slavery and forced labour. The European Convention goes further:

(1) No one shall be held in slavery or servitude.
(2) No one shall be required to perform forced or compulsory labour.

It was the European Court of Human Rights (ECtHR) that published guidance on how to interpret Article 4 and the prohibition of slavery, servitude and forced or compulsory labour (European Court of Human Rights, 2014).

The guidance demonstrates how the Court draws on the international instruments referred to earlier, unequivocally, using the 1926 Slavery Convention's definition of slavery. Forced labour then undergoes greater clarification and analysis. The European Council Guidance on Article 4 explains that forced or compulsory labour includes any *work* or *service* and is not limited to manual labour (and therefore potentially incorporates forced begging and forced criminal activities).

'Force' refers to control or constraint on the victim and compulsory refers to the imposition of 'any penalty'. That may include physical violence or restraint but may also include subtler forms, such as psychological coercion (which might include intimidation and threats based upon cultural values and beliefs or superstitions), or threats of violence or threat to denounce the victim to law enforcement or other authorities.

The development of human rights through these conventions has been a slow and complex process but has resulted in many of the fundamental principles that guide both legislation, policy and practice in safeguarding children and vulnerable people from exploitation, oppression and violence in the 21st century.

The evolution of anti-slavery legislation

It is case law that influences and shapes how domestic law should be applied which in turn informs policy, practice and procedures. Examples of international case law can be seen in Table 2.1. What constitutes relevant evidence for modern slavery informs how victims and perpetrators are identified, how perpetrators are to be disrupted, pursued and prosecuted, and how victims are protected and supported towards safety and recovery. It is case law that informs the statutory frameworks within which police, social workers, health professionals, NGOs and the business community must operate.

Case example: Siliadin v France (2005) 43 EHRR 287

Siliadin was a 15-year-old girl from Togo. She was brought to France by Mrs D, a French national of Togolese origin, on a tourist visa. It had been agreed that Siliadin would work at Mrs D's home until the cost of her airfare had been reimbursed and that Mrs D would enrol her in school and take care of her immigration matters. Instead, Mr and Mrs D took Siliadin's passport and forced her to work as an unpaid housemaid.

She was later 'lent' to Mr and Mrs B, who decided to 'keep her' as an unpaid housemaid and child caretaker, working 15-hour days, seven days a week. She was not paid, not sent to school and her immigration matters were never handled.

After a neighbour alerted France's Committee against Modern Slavery, Mr and Mrs B's home was raided and they were charged with (i) obtaining the performance of services without payment by taking advantage of a person's vulnerability or state of dependence under Article 225-13 of the Criminal Code (France) and (ii) subjecting an individual to working and living conditions

Table 2.1: Key international authorities

Issue	Case citation	Judgment
Forced/ compulsory labour	*Van der Mussele v Belgium* (8919/80) (1983) 11 WLUK 238; (1984) 6 E.H.R.R. 163; ECHR; 23 November 1983	The European Court of Human Rights held that a requirement for pupil lawyers to undertake pro bono work was not in breach of their right under Article 4(2) of the European Convention on Human Rights not to be required to perform forced or compulsory labour. At the material time, pupil lawyers in Belgium were required to accept a percentage of pro bono cases allocated to them during their three-year pupillage.
Servitude (Primary ECHR Authority)	*Siliadin v France* (2005) 43 EHRR 287	Servitude is an obligation to provide one's services that is imposed by the use of coercion.
Trafficking	*Rantsev v Cyprus* App No 25965/04 (ECtHR 7 January 2010)	The European Court of Human Rights unanimously ruled that human trafficking fell within the scope of Article 4 (prohibiting slavery, servitude and forced labour) of the *European Convention*. The Court clarified the positive obligations upon States to investigate allegations of trafficking and to implement measures to prevent and protect people from human trafficking.

incompatible with human dignity by taking advantage of a person's vulnerability or state of dependence under Article 225-14 of the Criminal Code (France).

Mr and Mrs B were convicted of violating Article 225-13 and sentenced to 12 months' imprisonment each, seven months of which was suspended, a fine of 100,000 francs and ordered to pay 100,000 francs in damages to Siliadin.

The Paris Court of Appeal overturned the convictions and acquitted the defendants. The Principal Public Prosecutor's Office refused to appeal the acquittal; however, Siliadin appealed the civil aspects of the decision. The Versailles Court of Appeal ruled that Article 225-13 had been violated and awarded Siliadin compensation for psychological trauma. In addition, the Paris Industrial Court awarded her EUR 33,049 in relation to arrears of salary, notice period and holiday leave.

Siliadin subsequently made an application to the ECtHR, claiming that France failed to comply with its positive obligation under Article 4, together with Article 1, of the European Convention on Human Rights (the 'ECHR') to put in place adequate criminal law provisions to prevent and effectively punish the perpetrators of slavery, servitude or forced or compulsory labour.

In its guidance on slavery, servitude, forced or compulsory labour and trafficking, the ECtHR explains 'With regard to the concept of "servitude", what is prohibited is "particularly serious forms of denial of freedom"'. It includes 'in addition to the obligation to perform certain services for others ... the obligation for the "serf" to live on another person's property and the impossibility of altering his condition'.

The Court underlined that domestic servitude is a specific offence, distinct from trafficking and exploitation and which involves a complex set of dynamics, involving both overt and more-subtle forms of coercion, to force compliance.

In *Siliadin v France* the Court considered that Siliadin was held in servitude because, in addition to the fact that she was required to perform forced labour, she was a minor with no resources, vulnerable and isolated with no means of living elsewhere than the home where she worked at their mercy and completely depended on them with no freedom of movement and no free time.

Three judgments by the ECtHR have provided definitional clarity and guidance concerning forced or compulsory labour, servitude and trafficking.

Forced or compulsory labour: *Van der Mussele v Belgium*

This case is notable perhaps for defining what is not forced or compulsory labour rather than what is. Belgian law provides that the Order of Advocates (Bar Association) makes provisions to assist people who need legal aid to have been provided representation by Pupil Advocates without payment. Van der Mussele, a pupil advocate, viewed this as forced or compulsory labour under

Article 4(2) of the UNCHR, a violation of Protocol 1 Article 1 and discrimination under Article 14. The Court did not agree.

The Court found no violation of Article 4: the free legal aid service Mr Van der Mussele was asked to provide was connected with his profession – he received certain advantages for it, such as the exclusive right to audience in the courts, and it contributed to his professional training; it was related to another Convention right (Art 6(1) the right to legal aid) and could be considered part of 'normal civic obligations' allowed under Article 4(3). Finally, being required to defend people without being paid for it did not leave Mr Van der Mussele without sufficient time for paid work.

Most UN Member States have ratified at least one of the core international instruments addressing human exploitation. If the ILO Convention of 1926 overtly made forced labour subject to the penal code of any jurisdiction in which it occurred, this convention and the Palermo Protocol situated trafficking of human beings within the context of serious and organised crime. Despite this, relatively few countries have opted to criminalise slavery, servitude, forced labour and slavery-like practices. The empirical analysis of the data from the Anti-Slavery Legislation Database[3] (Schwartz and Allain, 2020) found that, overall, only three States (2 per cent) do not have specific treaty obligations to prohibit slavery, servitude, forced labour, practices similar to slavery or trafficking in human beings (Bhutan, Tonga and Tuvalu), while 113 States (59 per cent) are required to prohibit all five (p 9).

In this analysis, Schwartz and Allain found that among UN members 94 States (49 per cent) appear not to have criminal legislation prohibiting slavery or the slave trade; 170 States (88 per cent) appear not to have criminalised the four institutions and practices similar to slavery; 180 States (93 per cent) appear not to have enacted legislative provisions criminalising servitude; 112 States (58 per cent) appear not to have put in place penal provisions for the punishment of forced labour. Nevertheless, the impact of the Palermo Protocol has been such that prohibition against trafficking of human beings has achieved almost complete

---

[3] The Anti-Slavery Legislation Database is hosted by the Anti-Slavery in Domestic Legislation Platform and compiles the national level, constitutional, criminal and labour legislation of all 193 UN Member States.

domestic implementation, with 185 of the 193 UN Member States (96 per cent) having penal sanctions in the context of this transnational crime (Schwartz and Allain, 2020).

Human trafficking

A practice that is inextricably linked to exploitation is trafficking of human beings: the generally accepted definition of trafficking of human beings was formed within the 'Protocol to Prevent, Suppress and Punish Trafficking in Persons, Especially Women and Children', better known as the 'Palermo Protocol'. This was one of three protocols that supplemented the United Nations Convention Against Transnational Organised Crime 2000. The Protocol defines trafficking thus:

(a) 'Trafficking in persons' shall mean the recruitment, transportation, transfer, harbouring or receipt of persons, by means of the threat or use of force or other forms of coercion, of abduction, of fraud, of deception, of the abuse of power or of a position of vulnerability or of the giving or receiving of payments or benefits to achieve the consent of a person having control over another person, for the purpose of exploitation. Exploitation shall include, at a minimum, the exploitation, forced labour or services, slavery or practices similar to slavery, servitude or the removal of organs;

(b) The consent of a victim of trafficking in persons to the intended exploitation set forth in subparagraph (a) of this Article shall be irrelevant where any of the means set forth in subparagraph (a) have been used;

(c) The recruitment, transportation, transfer, harbouring or receipt of a child for the purpose of exploitation shall be considered 'trafficking in persons' even if this does not involve any of the means set forth in subparagraph (a) of this article;

(d) 'Child' shall mean any person under 18 years of age. (United Nations, 2000)

This is an important, comprehensive and highly influential definition. It signified the movement towards recognising the link between human trafficking and slavery particularly where control, intimidation and severe power imbalances lead to slavery-like exploitation despite no actual rights of ownership being involved (Kara, 2011, p 125). But its birth within the Convention Against Transnational Organised Crime is significant. First, this definition is describing the transport of people, through whatever means, for the explicit purpose of exploitation, be that in the form of slavery, forced labour, servitude or some other form of exploitation. It extends the concept of 'force' to the recruitment and transportation *prior* to the exploitative activity. This effectively makes slavery, servitude and forced or compulsory labour a spectrum of exploitative activity that does not simply begin and end with a single user or controller of the victim, but incorporates potentially a chain or network of agents that gain from the exploitation (for example, as recruiter, transporters, facilitators who provide the means for the exploitation).

Case example: Rantsev v Cyprus and Russia

Oxana Rantsev was a 21-year-old Russian national. She died in unexplained circumstances after falling from a window of a private property in Cyprus in March 2001. She had arrived in Cyprus a few days earlier on a 'cabaret-artiste' visa, but had abandoned her work and lodging shortly after starting and had left a note to say she wanted to return to Russia. The manager of the cabaret found her some days later, and took her to the central police station in the early morning and asked them to detain her as an illegal immigrant. The police had contacted the immigration authorities who gave instructions that Oxana was not to be detained and that her employer, who was responsible for her, was to pick her up and bring her to the immigration office. The manager collected Oxana and took her to private premises, where he had also remained. Her body was then found in the street below the apartment. A bedspread had been looped through the railing of the balcony suggesting that she had fallen while trying to escape.

An inquest held in Cyprus concluded that Oxana had died in circumstances resembling an accident while attempting to escape from an apartment in which she was a guest, but that there was no evidence of foul play.

After her body had been repatriated, the Russian authorities considered, in the light of a further autopsy, that the verdict of the inquest was unsatisfactory; the Cypriot authorities stated that it was final and refused to carry out any additional investigations unless the Russian authorities had evidence of criminal activity. No steps were taken by either the Russian or Cypriot authorities to interview two young women living in Russia whom it is believed had worked with Oxana at the cabaret and could testify to sexual exploitation taking place there. What followed was a long and protracted argument between Cyprus and Russia over the investigation of Oxana's death and the verdict of the inquest.

Oxana's father, Nikolay Rantsev appealed to the ECtHR. He argued that there was no adequate investigation of Oxana's death and that the Cypriot police had failed to protect her while she was alive. In addition, he argued that the Cypriot justice system, despite being aware of the extent of trafficking for sexual exploitation in Cyprus, had failed to punish those that had exposed Oxana to the abuse and exploitation that culminated in her death.

The ECtHR found that Cyprus had failed to protect her from being trafficked and unlawfully detained prior to her death and had failed to adequately investigate her death.

> The Cypriot authorities' investigation into the death had been unsatisfactory in a number of ways: inconsistencies in the evidence had been left unresolved; relevant witnesses had not been questioned; little had been done to investigate events at the police station and, in particular, possible corruption on the part of the police; the applicant had not been able to participate effectively in the proceedings; and the Cypriot authorities had refused a Russian offer of assistance that would have enabled them to obtain the testimony of two important witnesses. (ECtHR judgment, 10 May 2010)

As Oxana was a Russian national, the Court also found Russia (as the state of origin) had failed to investigate the way in which she had been trafficked from her home in Russia to Cyprus:

> The Court made it clear that Member States were required to take necessary and available steps to secure relevant evidence, whether or not it was located on their territory, particularly in a case such as the instant one, in which both States were parties to a convention providing for mutual assistance in criminal matters. (ECtHR judgment, 10 May 2010)

A fault line in global anti-slavery strategies

Despite progress in the development of the language, definition and explanation for exploitative behaviours remains contested, unclear and under-theorised (Heys, 2023). When the efforts of legislators to incorporate international conventions and protocols and obligations into domestic legislation are looked at closely, a major fault line in the global response to modern slavery emerges with startling clarity.

My colleagues and I have argued elsewhere (Green, Heys, and Barlow, forthcoming) that this contestation manifests itself in what may be described as a fault line between the framing of the problem on one hand as interpersonal victimisation and criminal justice (as exemplified by the Palermo Protocol) on the other hand, as a problem of human rights, migration and global economic forces. This results in a tendency to rely upon examples of exploitative practices (such as suppression of wages and employee rights, extension of working hours, human trafficking, modern slavery and unfree labour) without ever providing a coherent definition of exploitation, or recognising the conditions that cause it to occur. In other words, the current debate is focused on identifying the types and locations of exploitation, rather than explain why it happens in different places at different times (Green, Heys, and Barlow, forthcoming).

The *Rantsev* judgment has been an important authority for advocates working in the field of human rights, trafficking of human beings and modern slavery because it has stated that human trafficking is a violation of Article 4 of the ECHR; namely:

- No one shall be held in slavery or servitude.
- No one shall be required to perform forced or compulsory labour.

The Court stated:

> There can be no doubt that trafficking threatens the human dignity and fundamental freedoms of its victims and cannot be considered compatible with a democratic society and the values expounded in the Convention. In view of its obligation to interpret the Convention in light of present-day conditions, the Court considers it unnecessary to identify whether the treatment about which the applicant complains constitutes 'slavery', 'servitude' or 'forced and compulsory labour.' Instead, the Court concludes that trafficking itself ... falls within the scope of Article 4 of the Convention.

The ECtHR is rarely called upon to consider the application of Article 4. Prior to *Rantsev*, it had only previously been called to do so in *Van der Mussele* and *Siliadin*. If the former judgment indicates that the case of aggrieved lawyer did not amount to any sensible concept of slavery and forced labour envisaged by Article 4, the *Siliadin* judgment had been criticised for its narrow construal of the definition of slavery under Article 4 and in so doing relied on the definition of 'slavery' in the Slavery Convention 1926 ('the status or condition of a person over whom any or all of the powers attaching to the right of ownership are exercised') while not really considering the legal definition of human trafficking (Kara, 2011) established by the Palermo Protocol and the Council of Europe Convention on Action Against Trafficking in Human Beings, despite the ample evidence in the *Siliadin* case.

Kara (2011, p 125) suggests that in *Rantsev* the Court overcomes the first criticism of *Siliadin* by clearly acknowledging new and evolving forms of slavery. Allain counterpoints Kara's position arguing that *Rantsev*:

muddied the waters of the normative elements of human exploitation but also muddied the jurisprudence of Article 4 ... the Court determined that trafficking was based on the definition of slavery. It will be recalled that it 'considers that trafficking in human beings, by its very nature and aim of exploitation, is based on the exercise of powers attaching to the right of ownership' ... thus following the logic of the development of the Court's jurisprudence regarding Article 4, it must be understood that, legally speaking, trafficking cannot transpire within Europe as there exists no legal right to own a person within the Council of Europe. (Allain, 2010, p 557)

Stoyanova (2012) also argues that while the Court is concerned in *Rantsev* with the concept of human trafficking, it offers no meaningful legal analysis as to the elements of the human trafficking definition, and that the adoption of the human trafficking framework implicates the ECtHR in anti-immigration and anti-prostitution agenda.

Why assumptions, definitions and language matter

To be legislated against, trafficking and exploitation through various forms of slavery and labour exploitation need to be problematised to be defined. Once defined, policy responses can be formulated (Broad and Turnbull, 2018). Law and policy serve to characterise trafficking of human beings and modern slavery by identifying a range of regulatory frameworks to resolve problems or threats to the stability, well-being and cohesion of a society. Inevitably this is based upon a set of assumptions about the nature and causes of the problem, what regulation might achieve, how the goals of regulation will be achieved and thresholds for intervention, sanction and systems of adjudication (Fudge, 2018).

The 1926 Slavery Convention criminalised slavery, servitude and forced or compulsory labour and the Palermo Protocol together with the United Nations Convention against Transnational Organized Crime emphasise trafficking as a criminal activity and imply that it is primarily an activity of organised crime.

In *Rantsev* the ECtHR has not only linked directly the practice of human trafficking to slavery, servitude and forced labour but has made trafficking itself an act of slavery. It is this fusion of concepts which Allain argues has 'muddied the waters' and the effect has impacted upon political rhetoric, scholarly research and debate, policy development and created a serious fault line in the field of counter trafficking and exploitation of human beings.

The ECtHR judgment in *Rantsev* means that various legal strands of definitions of human trafficking and modern slavery that have been incorporated into international and domestic law and anti-trafficking and anti-slavery policies emphasise a perpetrator exercising the right of ownership. This means treating the victim as property: it incorporates notions of possession and coercion and a lack of agency for victims where different methods of coercion and control are applied (Landman, 2018, p 146). Criminal and human rights lawyer Alexandra Malangone does not entirely agree with this position, illustrating from a practitioner point of view how these waters have been 'muddied'.

> I tend to disagree here. The threshold has not been set in *Rantsev* that unless the right of ownership is exercised, THB [trafficking of human beings] situation as such fails to constitute violation of Article 4 ... maybe in practise some actors deliberately choose to interpret the *Rantsev* judgment as such but in my view – stemming also from the exchange of views with the judges of the ECtHR when I was a member of GRETA – judges who decided this case – nothing in *Rantsev* envisages exclusivity of such scenarios when contemplating THB as an Article 4 violation. Perhaps it is more convenient to interpret that 'right of ownership' is required to raise the threshold to say who is trafficked and who is not (or which situation constitutes THB and which not – meaning for example, unless you are not tied to a radiator and physically prevented to leave there is no THB) but certainly in the legislation per se as well as interpretative guidance to *Rantsev*, there is no requirement for exploitation to be so severe as to amount to the exercise of the right of

ownership and neither is the *Rantsev* judgment saying that. Most European THB Criminal Code provisions state only: ... 'for the purpose of exploitation', 'as a minimum constitutes' and some listing taxatively various forms and many leaving also the formulation 'and any other form of exploitation' (open for judicial practise) in their penal code definitions. (Malangone, 2024)

Anti-slavery policies are situated within wider crime policies which are largely developed by (inter) national bureaucratic and legal institutions, guided by overarching definitions (Broad and Turnbull, 2018, p 121).

This governmental framing of the problem and top-down development of policy and regulation focuses less on why and how trafficking and modern slavery occurs than whether or not it has occurred, by whom it was perpetrated and what the appropriate sanctions should be, conceptualising trafficking and modern slavery as a criminal justice matter (Barlow, 2022, p 150) which in turn means that there is an assumption of a crime, a perpetrator and a victim. However, constructing trafficking and slavery in this way renders these acts as crimes against the state rather than against the person and in legislating, the state decides who is a perpetrator and who is a vicim.

Central to this framing of trafficking and slavery is the notion of force or coercive control of victims who have no realistic option to change their circumstances. This framing has been criticised for making the plight of exploited workers in the 21st century analogous to the experience of chattel slaves, thereby making the historic Atlantic slave trade and trafficking of human beings synonymous. Gross and Thomas (2017) coined the term 'slavery-trafficking nexus' and suggest that it may:

> constrict understanding of contemporary human vulnerability as a problem of immigration and labor law (Gross and Thomas, 2017, p 102) in which other forms of exploitation which may be at play within trafficking such as peonage, removal of organs, surrogacy, begging and forced criminality but

involving the exploitation of people who may not be considered 'slaves'. (Allain, 2010)

O'Connell Davidson has been a strong proponent of this view. She rejects the suggestion that trafficking of human beings can be separated from other violations of human and labour rights, arguing that 'discourse on "trafficking as modern slavery" closes down, rather than opens up, possibilities for effective political struggle against the restrictions, exploitation and injustices that many groups of migrants experience' (O'Connell Davidson, 2010, p 245). This means that a state can simultaneously enact draconian laws on migration and de-regulation of business and trade so that opportunities for exploitative practices (for example, wage suppression, unrestricted working hours and unsafe working conditions) are created (Green, Heys, and Barlow, forthcoming) and anti-trafficking and anti-slavery legislation such as the UK's Modern Slavery Act 2015.

Conclusion

A vast amount of political and sholarly effort has been deployed over decades to define and describe a problem and in so doing develop top-down responses based upon often flawed assumptions about victims, perpetrators and motivations. These definitions influence policy and practice by stating what is trafficking and modern slavery and therefore who is or is not a victim with empirically weak thresholds by which those who must make decisions about investigation, protection of victims and the pursuit and prosecution of perpetrators must evaluate evidence. But how can 'exploitation' be evidenced in the context of establishing whether a human trafficking offence has been committed?

I propose we put aside these definitions for now and instead of trying to establish what trafficking and modern slavery is, we investigate why and how trafficking and modern slavery happens and why it affects specific populations in different contexts over time.

The historical efforts to define exploitation and its relationship to trafficking and modern slavery demonstrate how exploitation is currently an elastic concept, often located in political, economic and moral discourses, as well as crime and justice debates. This elasticity explains the preference for the language of 'human trafficking' and 'modern slavery' by academics and campaigners whose focus is to raise awareness and improve the international responses by relying on extreme examples of exploitation (Bales, 2012). However, the criminalisation of some types of behaviour is often criticised on the grounds it serves contemporary transatlantic economic and political expediencies, perpetuating the institutionalisation of global exploitative labour practices and reifying the divide between migrants and non-migrants (O'Connell Davidson, 2010). Both these perspectives challenge the status quo in different ways, but both have the inadvertent effect of polarising the debate (Green, Heys, and Barlow, forthcoming). This polarising effect has contributed to, if not created, the fault line in the framing of the problem. The criminal justice characterisation of the problem is therefore one side of the fault line with those who see it as a human rights and labour relations issue on the other.

To overcome this problem in the rest of this book, I will draw on recent work with my colleagues Simon Green and Alicia Heys (2023) and our argument that, if defined clearly, exploitation is a social practice that can be studied independently of any legal criteria and thus avoids the danger of either ethnocentrism (or cultural imperialism) or ideological doctrine and looks to the disadvantage that leads to the exploitation. We proposed a tripartite definition comprising of the following components:

(1) power and privilege;
(2) unfair benefit; and
(3) disadvantage.

Power, privilege and disadvantage are governed by structural conditions that shape who is in a position to gain profit from subjecting other people to harm/abuse. These all exist in a constantly adapting ecosystem in which specific circumstances give rise to specific opportunities to exploit (or not) and to be exploited (or not). Trafficking, slavery, servitude, forced and compulsory labour, and exploitation refer to patterns of behaviour that emerge from transactions defined by the power relationships between people in different contexts. Whether a person is the exploited or the exploiter, these transactional relationships depend on the needs, goals, knowledge and experience that motivate their decisions and actions. These needs, goals and decisions to act are context-specific and fluctuate over time.

3

Trafficking, modern slavery and exploitation: degrees of organisation

Trafficking of human beings is the movement of people for the purposes of exploitation. In the UK, the primary legislation binds trafficking human beings for the purpose of exploitation to the concept and processes of modern slavery. However, what constitutes modern slavery is not always clear-cut or easy to identify (van der Watt and van der Westhuizen, 2017). Exploitation is a spectrum of harmful abuse to which people are subjected in different contexts (sexual, labour, criminal and so on) and, through this, financial/material profit or some other gain is secured which is the main goal of all this enterprise. The presence of the other two constitutive elements of trafficking of human beings (THB) as a crime are present too (actions plus means) establishes whether we are concerned with trafficking for the purpose of exploitation, or a form of exploitation that does not include trafficking.

Despite the detail and breadth of academic and clinical knowledge and experience, strategic responses have been confusing and reactive. Recent attempts to formulate typologies of exploitation, such as the UK Home Office 'A Typology of Modern Slavery Offences in the UK' (Cooper et al, 2017), the International Labour Organization's Operational Indicators of Human Trafficking in Human Bings (International Labour Organization, 2009) and the UNODC Trafficking Indicators (United Nations Office on Drugs and Crime), can be distracting and counterproductive.

Within this chapter I will examine the aetiology of exploitation through slavery, servitude, forced labour and other exploitative practices in relation to constructs of organised crime. A concept of the 'degrees of organisation' in relation to trafficking and exploitation is presented to describe and explain its presentation and modalities. I will use a series of case studies to illustrate the research evidence that has been cited and the argument that is being made.

I conclude the chapter by establishing the need for a sound concept of exploitation as a mode of abuse, built upon a solid theoretical foundation to take account of, and make better utilisation of, existing resources, measures and remedies.

Conceptualising exploitation

Definitions and categories of exploitative and criminal behaviour are perceived as useful – necessary even – because they provide a structure for exploring motive and victimology. It is important, however, to be mindful of the problems in reducing criminal, exploitative or otherwise abusive behaviour to a series of types with the potential for these to be interpreted as a prescription for dealing with a problem.

Patterns of exploitation are diverse in terms of the exploitative activities – who might be exploited by whom and under what circumstances. There is an overlap between types of exploitation – for example, sexual exploitation, domestic servitude, forced labour and criminal exploitation – and people may be exploited for more than one purpose. Detection of such exploitation is hampered by uncertainty regarding the nature and interpretation of evidence. Prosecution can be difficult due to the perception of witnesses as unreliable, particularly when they are child witnesses and victims of trafficking themselves may find the criminal justice process terrifying (Nawala, 2023). People may not recognise the coercive nature of their relationships which may be especially salient when exploitation emerges from within the victim's own family (for example, when perpetrated by the parents, spouse, sibling or cousin). Similarly, social learning processes and the behaviour over a period of time may condition a victim of abuse and exploitation to behave in a specific way (ECPAT UK, 2010). The way in which they perceive the nature, conditions and purpose of the activities in which they are engaged may mean that an abused and exploited person does not hold a construct of themselves as victim.

Work, labour and exploitation

As my colleagues Simon Green and Alicia Heys and I have discussed elsewhere (Green, Heys, and Barlow, forthcoming), concepts of exploitation, especially in relation to work and labour, have been found to be vulnerable to the bias caused by cultural relativism. By way of example, the Western discourse on child labour in India has been criticised for this precise bias.

Raman (2000) draws a conceptual distinction between 'work' and 'labour' and proposes that work may be that which is done within the home or family environment and contributes to the home life through the shared completion of domestic chores. Labour, he contends, involves payment of wages in exchange for work or service. If such distinctions are drawn within the child's family or community, any services or labour that contributes to family life is not experienced, nor labelled, as exploitative or problematic as the child is making a valued and positive contribution to the family's survival.

Article 32 of the United Nations Convention on the Rights of the Child (UNCRC) establishes the child's right to be protected from economic exploitation and from performing work that is likely to be hazardous; or to interfere with the child's education; or is harmful to the child's spiritual, moral or social development. Poor children may thus be compelled by circumstances to work in order to meet their own and their family's survival needs. This work may involve exposure to unhealthy or outright dangerous conditions. Nevertheless, Raman argues that what constitutes 'exploitation' and 'harmful' may be somewhat relative concepts which vary across cultures and societies. This may be at odds with Western standards so that such work is seen as having its own value and status: it not only contributes to the child's own family survival and viability, but facilitates greater integration into wider family and community.

Ballet et al (2002) take up this issue with regard to begging, offering three typologies of children that are engaged in begging:

(1) Children That Are Coerced by Their Parents. These parents forced the children to handover all the proceeds. Violence was used against the children and the children tended to be younger.

(2) Children That Spent the Proceeds Directly on Food. The coercion into begging was largely a result of neglect. Such children were also likely to develop other, more lucrative forms of criminal activity as a source of income.

(3) Children Who Had at Least One Sick or Disabled Parent. These children tended to hand over their proceeds. Coercion was largely psychological: the child was working in the belief that the family were dependent upon them and that if they did not earn money the family would disintegrate.

The typologies offer a potentially useful model to differentiate begging contexts according to the nature and degree of coercion applied to the child but the neglect to which Raman refers is implicitly a conscious (or wilful) act of omission on the part of the parents. Neglect as a form or process of maltreatment is complicated and may not always be intentional but a consequence of circumstances (for example, extreme material poverty and poverty of opportunity) and impairment of a parent's ability or capacity to care for their child. In Ballet's typology each type of child came from extreme poverty. The main difference seems to be whether the begging resulted from violent and psychological coercion or neglect.

Ballet et al (2002) explore the family narratives that support or condone begging. They also identify a complicating factor in describing contexts of begging resulting from the United Nations Children's Fund (UNICEF) differentiation between 'on street' children and 'of the street' children. 'On street' children are engaged in some form of work, which might include begging but live with at least one parent and return to some form of accommodation after work. 'Of the street' children are homeless and living on the streets at great risk. These children are runaways or have been abandoned. Some have migrated in search of work. Thus, a significant proportion of the children that are begging may already have experienced abuse and neglect as well as extreme poverty, and yet their experiences of safe attachments and affiliation are poorer than those that are begging to support their family. In this analysis, the relevance of social history, development and environment become salient in understanding the nature and trajectory of the child worker's experience and the diversity of experiences and trajectories among children of superficially similar demographics.

Ballet et al's typology demonstrates the need for survival as being antecedents to the exploitative activity. Whether or not a child is engaged in legitimate work and labour, the context to their activities is an integral part of their socialisation: the family and community is of greater importance; it is where they are affiliated and learn adult roles in a variety of situations that 'integrate them into the family and the community' (Raman, 2000, p 4057). This is something of a counterpoint to the UNCRC Article 28, which establishes the child's right to education but assumes that the only suitable place other than home, where healthy psycho-social development can be nurtured, is in school. Ballet et al's point here is that the necessity for work and labour, due to the fundamental physical needs that are food, shelter, warmth, safety and security (Maslow, [1943] 2014), renders a school-based education irrelevant. The practical survival skills that the child learns in these contexts are vital and, in fact, formal education within school, away from home, is in effect a threat to the safety of the child and the stable equilibrium of the family.

Coercion, control and circumstances

Raman's differentiation between work and labour, and Ballet et al's analysis of family rationales behind begging, raise an issue regarding the concept of exploitation and the relationship between exploitation and the use of force: one interpretation of 'force' is that this incorporates an act, or series of intentional actions, that compel an individual to do something for, or on behalf of, the controlling other. There may, therefore, be physical coercion and psychological coercion (for example, blackmail, threats) the victim complies with because they will be, or believe that they will be, harmed or perceive it to be right that they should undertake or participate in the activity. Whether or not physical violence is used, the person is compelled by an act of commission on the part of the controlling person. However, with reference back to Ballet et al's typologies 2 and 3, the activity that the person engages in may be forced by circumstance because of neglect by the person on whom the victim is dependent or controlled by; an intentional act of omission.

Many of Raman's arguments may apply in other regions where the poorest communities may lack the resources that allow them to access and participate in formal education, forcing them to seek paying labour and rendering them vulnerable to exploitation that may be either illegal or criminal.

Case example: Operation RASTRELLI

D was a 19-year-old woman from Romania. She and her family lived in extreme poverty. Like many of her contemporaries at the time, with few opportunities and very limited personal resources, she embarked upon sex work to earn money and support her family. I shall discuss D's experiences shortly, but I asked her about her experience of school and her hopes and aspirations. She told me that she attended school until the age of 15 when compulsory education ended. She had enjoyed sport, drama and had learned a little English but left school so that she could help her mother at home and care for her younger siblings. She said that she would have liked to have stayed in education, maybe to have gone to college but that was never an option for girls such as her, from her background. Under these conditions she decided to spend what little money she had to travel to London to work in prostitution. Her rationale was that she could probably work in better conditions, earn more and therefore leave sex work more quickly and return home.

The senior investigating officer in Operation RASTRELLI had visited Romania and the region from which D came. He described the extreme poverty in which she and her contemporaries had grown up. Sex work was so common as the only means by which women Like D could make ends meet that within the community there was almost no stigma attached to it. D's decision to travel to

London to work as a prostitute may seem risky to most ordinary people but if we understand her rationale, the circumstances under which her decision was made, it is rational, even realistic. The sources of information that she relied upon to make her decision, however, may have been limited to her own life experience, what she has seen or heard elsewhere and the beliefs that she had formed about how the world should work.

Exploitation and organised crime

Recent cases, such as Operation FORT in the UK and JOKER/ KRONE in Europe, have demonstrated the enormous profits that are to be made by organised crime groups (OCGs) that are exploiting vulnerable people. The activities that may constitute the trafficking and exploitation are frequently similar to, and may overlap with, other forms of criminality that constitute, or are associated with, organised crime. To understand one is to take a substantial step towards understanding the other. The problems of defining and describing organised crime are manifold but Newburn (2012) cites critical criminologist James Chambliss in summarising the problems that are inherent in forming constructs and definitions of organised crime: 'one of the reasons we fail to understand organised crime is because we put crime into a category that is separate from normal business activity'.

Methods for THB vary according to the degrees of organisation of the traffickers, their motivation, their objectives and their physical, social, cultural, political and economic environments. Indeed, Shelley (2010) describes how business models of OCGs engaged in THB reflect traditional business practices in the offenders' country of origin. She argues that today's modern 'slave trade' is shaped by cultural, geographic and economic forces, and these influences coalesce to create a conducive environment in which patterns of exploitation emerge and are maintained (Green, Heys, and Barlow, forthcoming).

A similar observation is made by Fatić (1999) who explains how the dismantling of the authoritarian Eastern European infrastructure was simultaneous with the abolition of the Communist-era ideology of control and oppression. This, he reasons, meant a legitimisation of the acquisition of wealth, or at least the opportunities and means to acquire wealth, regardless of the effects such means may have upon individuals or communities, or the morality of the enterprise. This set of values and social attitudes, as expressed by Fatić, contributes to an environment that is conducive to the emergence of exploitation and human trafficking as an activity or output of organised crime. His proposal suggests that organised crime needs to be understood not just in its economic context, but its historical and cultural context also. He highlights the ways in which prevailing socio-cultural factors contribute to the neutralisation of crimes such as criminal exploitation by offenders, society and potentially the exploited person.

While his explanation for the emergence of OCGs offers some worthwhile insights into the possible motivation for individuals to engage in such criminality (and the benefits of criminal affiliation), Fatić (1999) clearly rejects the concept of a 'Russian Mafia'. The appeal of the 'Russian Mafia' concept reflects the dominance of the American model of organised crime, or syndicated crime, in both popular and criminological understandings in this area (Newburn, 2012). These concepts are rooted in Cressey's (1969) influential book *Theft of the Nation* in which he described the activities and structure of the Cosa Nostra and Sicilian Mafia in the US. Cressey's work has been criticised for the fact that its sources are limited.[1] However, a point that is often overlooked is his warning, echoed by Chambliss, that organised crime reflects normal business but furthermore implicates society in general, stating: 'Our society tends, both popularly and scientifically to view the criminal's behaviour as a problem of individual maladjustment, not of his participation in social system' (Cressey, 1969). He goes on to suggest that such organised crime flourishes only for as long as a community or society is willing to tolerate it.

Criminal justice systems tend to be primarily concerned with whether the crime was committed but is less concerned with the biographical elements of an offender's motivation for committing the crime. Thus, petty street crime and begging may

---

[1] Cressey relies heavily upon the evidence of a single source (Joseph 'Joe Cargo' Valachi) and official data such as phone tap transcripts and other covert recordings.

be perceived by society in general as a 'nuisance' and those that are seen to perpetrate these crimes are labelled as delinquent. By labelling them as delinquent, society situates the problem with the individual, a narrow focus that avoids examining the activities and routines, values and attitudes of society that create the opportunity for such criminality and fails to recognise where organised and networked exploitation is occurring; for example, by forcing people to beg or engage in criminality on the behalf of another or group of others.

Case example: Operation GOLF

> The children identified as exploited in the UK during Operation GOLF were involved in begging and petty street crime. Despite the low level, unsophisticated appearance of these crimes, the criminals that were controlling the children (and some of their parents) were engaged in a wider range of criminal enterprises. The GOLF investigation led to 18 people who were subsequently arrested following raids on 34 homes in Tandarei, in southeast Romania. The arrests took place in an area of the town that had seen a dramatic rise in new, unexplained prosperity. This sudden wealth in the area bought residents luxury homes and expensive cars.
>
> In addition to the arrests, the operation recovered and seized four AK47 rifles, twelve hunting rifles, twelve shotguns that included military grade weapons, and six handguns. Large amounts of cash, high value cars and luxury homes were seized along with strong evidence that linked the ring leaders to crime in the UK and other EU Countries. (Anti-Slavery International, 2010)

In this case, the town of Tandarei had benefitted from the activities of the OCG and therefore may have had a vested interest in tolerating or ignoring how this wealth was generated. It is even possible that while welcoming the gains, the issue of child exploitation and trafficking could be deflected by the citizens of Tandarei as a problem of the Roma Community.

Identifying and describing: the problem of typologies of organised crime groups

Alach (2011) recalls how, when the mafia began to emerge, conceptual frameworks of organised crime were based upon slim evidence, preconceptions and prejudice. Cressey (1969), making the same observation, referred to the 'scapegoating' of Italian Americans. Types of organised crime and crime groups or networks can become 'conglomerated under labels of convenience' but seldom any defining characteristics (Alach, 2011, p 56); for example, Russian/Italian mafia, motorcycle gangs, paedophile rings, drug cartels, street gangs and so on. A similar process of scapegoating or victim blaming can simultaneously occur – for example: victims of child sexual exploitation are perceived as difficult teenage girls from care homes, trafficking is a foreign practice, victims are illegal migrants who still have a better standard of living in the destination country than they would at home, regardless of the cruelty of their situation. This situates trafficking and exploitation as organised crime with 'the other' (Levi, 1998) but does little to describe the nature of the criminality, or what makes it organised apart from the fact that it is a shared criminal enterprise that suggests at least some cooperation.

Subsequent policies have tended to dilute the analyses of Cressey and some of his predecessors, and ignore their warnings; re-defining organised crime and focusing on identification and disruption of OCGs and networks with ever more criminal legislation without addressing the systemic processes. These processes create the criminal opportunities, and facilitate and sustain the criminal enterprises.

At least in part, then, the difficulty in defining organised crime and the identification of OCGs may be attributed to its diversity and expansiveness (Scheptycki, 2003). It can also be difficult to clearly demarcate where illicit activities interface with licit activities; the aims and objectives of a crime group may be similar to (and even complement) the aims and objectives of legitimate businesses and social policy (Cressey, 1969; Scheptycki, 2003; Shelley, 2010). The nature of organised crime can vary in terms of the criminal activities involved, the sophistication with which it is conceived and executed and the extent of mutual cooperation and partnership between perpetrators. It is also highly adaptive: flux is as normal in illegal markets as it is in legal ones and is a challenge for any entrepreneur or enterprise, some of which are peripheral and ephemeral (Edwards and Gill, 2004). This makes the context of the criminality highly adaptive and mobile.

Despite these difficulties there is growing international consensus regarding some broad criteria for organised criminal activity: there must be three or more perpetrators working together over a period involving logistics (for example, movement of goods or, more commonly, money).

The definition used by the UK National Crime Agency and Europol is: 'Organised crime can be defined as serious crime planned, coordinated and conducted by people working together on a continuing basis. Their motivation is often, but not always, financial gain. Organised criminals working together for a particular criminal activity or activities are called an organised crime group' (National Crime Agency, 2015).

This seems clear and concise but, rather like a fading dream, loses coherence the closer it is examined. Serious crime may not be too difficult to conceptualise.

(1) Crimes such as murder, robbery and theft are single event crimes and well defined and generally accepted across cultures, faiths and societies as in and of themselves, wrong.

(2) Other behaviours become criminal because they are prohibited e.g. prostitution, drug dealing, bribery, and gambling. The behaviours may be outlawed, constrained or tolerated under certain circumstances, contravention of which is generally accepted as a crime even though the definitions may be less clear.

(3) Certain offences tend to be associated with organised crime such as trafficking of drugs, weapons and human beings, loan sharking, extortion and intimidation, counterfeiting and rigging sports events. (Finckenauer, 2005)

Nevertheless, any of these crimes may be undertaken by a group or an individual. The nature and range of criminal activity that may be found under the umbrella of organised crime is, by contrast, extremely diverse: one activity may be required to support or facilitate another (for example, money laundering to dispose of the gains of sexual exploitation through prostitution or forced criminality, such as cannabis cultivation and drug dealing). In the context of criminal exploitation of children, trafficking is a specific criminal offence that enables or facilitates the criminal exploitation, which is a process that facilitates another type of crime. The output of the exploitation may not be exclusive – children that are exploited in order to commit property or drug crimes may also be used for sexual exploitation, forced labour and domestic servitude. The exploitation may not be the main criminal activity of the individual or group but used to generate income to enable the financing of other projects or cooperation with other criminals and groups.

Sellin (1963) conceptualised organised crime as business enterprises that exist and operate much like any other enterprise. The key difference is that their activities are either in and of themselves illegal or use illegal means to maximise profit. By extension, this means that while criminal enterprises may not be constrained by the statutory rules (and inherent costs) of legitimate business governance, they also encounter problems that *do not* occur for legitimate businesses and may be insurmountable without collusion or cooperation with other criminals,[2] service providers or officials. The inclusion of these other agents adds complexity to the criminal organisation (Perrow, 1999).

The service providers or officials may be corrupt and collusive facilitators or quite ignorant that their services are being used to facilitate a criminal enterprise. Therefore, the criminal intent may conceivably lie with a lone actor; for example, a fraudster such as Charles Ponzi.[3] Although Ponzi's activity was criminal, he required victim participation and had to utilise legal systems (exploiting a weakness in the international reply coupon system) and institutions, such as banks, to succeed. This type of criminal

---

[2]   Italian-American Mafiosi today play a key role in criminal dispute settlement – they are trusted because they are a criminal group and their reputation for violence and discipline.

[3]   Ponzi schemes: fraudulent investment scams offering high returns within a short time frame. Charles Ponzi offered a false investment scheme, based on a form of arbitrage, which offered investors a 50 per cent return in 45 days. In reality he was using the money paid by later investors to pay out to early investors.

enterprise is a serious and lucrative fraud that requires planning but can be undertaken alone without the assistance of a group of like-minded criminals cooperating in the enterprise. Nevertheless, there is a network of active participants who may or may not know, or suspect, they are involved in a criminal enterprise.

Sellin's (1963) conclusion that organised crime can be conceptualised as a business enterprise is adopted by Finckenauer (2005) who points out that the phenomenon cannot be understood in terms of a crime, or crimes, but rather the purpose of the crime and aim, objectives and motivations of the organisation involved in the criminality. It is the nature and degree of the organisation and the results that count. To adapt Maltz's (1976) example of a simple numbers racket to the context of human trafficking, trafficking is a single type of criminal activity and is often based upon victim participation (perhaps beginning with illicit migration facilitated by an offer from the traffickers). If violence or the threat of violence is used to recruit, coerce or control the victim and ensure collusion from others it is also a violence-based criminal activity.

Case example: Operation GOLF – a violence-based organised crime group

Many of the child victims in Operation GOLF were found to have multiple cigarette burns, indicative of the degree of physical abuse exerted in their coercion and control. The nature of the coercion and control of children in this case appears to constitute torture; that is, the inflicting of intense pain, degrading and inhuman treatment: the children had cigarette burns on the parts of their body that were hidden under clothing. Such a sadistic form of child abuse seems gratuitous to the objective of gaining compliance from a child in earning money from crime and begging. Therefore, while the primary motivation for the criminal exploitation of children in this case is clearly the substantial profits to be made, the case needs to be further understood in terms of motivations towards violence and physical abuse or degrading and humiliating treatment to gain clearer insights into individual perpetrators of the abuse and the functioning of an OCG.

GOLF showed that there can be also a blurring of boundaries between who are criminal, those who are victims and those who are facilitators of the exploitation. The Local Safeguarding Children Board Notification suggested that while some of the adults were criminal members of an OCG, other adults were coerced into involvement, possibly providing and controlling their own children in the exploitation as a consequence of their own submission to coercion and control by others.

Sellin suggests that if, in addition, payments are made to border officials or other law enforcement officers, an OCG's business is corruption-based. Maltz asserts the importance of these distinctions in the evaluation of the type of organised crime or criminality if it is going to lead to effective prevention, disruption, investigation, prosecution and protection of victims.

Case example: Operation JOKER/KRONE – a corruption-based organised crime network

Corruption was a key strategy of the organised crime network (OCN) targetted by Operation JOKER/KRONE in 2022. It was the means of covering the illegal cigarette business that Jozef Kertész, a fuel entrepreneur from the village of Vlčany, paid bribes to people from the financial administration (KUFS).

KUFS appeared to be investigating illegal cigarette factories and then arresting and charging migrant workers. This would simply lead to their expulsion, but at the same time generated false statistics for 'resolved cases' of illicit migration and illegal workers. This provided further cover for the Head of KUFS, Ľudovít Makó, who was taking bribes for each truck full of illegal cigarettes, linked to the wider 'Czech-Slovak' part of the international illegal drug business, headed by Vilém Kováč.

Some of the bribes were personally delivered by Kertész's partner from the tobacco company, Gabriel Biherez. According to the prosecutor, Kertész should have paid out almost half a million euros between 2016 and 2020. The amount of the bribes is indicative of the volume of illegal cigarettes that left the Vozokany factory. The production of cigarettes for the illegal market was so great and returning such massive profits, that it was convenient to pay these considerable amounts of bribe money. Linked with the profits coming from the drug business, the corruption fees and the fees linked to recruitment, transportation and living costs of workers were considered as collateral only by the criminals and the factory workers did not receive any payment at all.

It is perhaps more helpful to consider organised crime as an adjective, describing a pattern of behaviour or activity rather than as a noun 'organised crime' which suggests a tidy concept or idea with a clear definition (Finckenauer, 2005; Alac, 2011); organised crime comprises a range of criminal activities and facilitators.

Information communication technology, the World Wide Web, and 'digital trafficking' and exploitation

The International Telecommunications Union (ITU) is the UN's source of Internet use statistics. According to the ITU's report for 2020, there were 63,504,106 users in the UK alone. This equates to 93.6 per cent of the population. The UK's National Crime Agency threat assessment of 2019 identified cybercrime as among the most significant crime and security threats, and identified it as the primary facilitator in child exploitation. Musto and Boyd (2014) examined the specific human trafficking–technology nexus both as a facilitator of human trafficking and as a means of disruption of trafficking. They argued that ICT is both a source and a solution to the problem of human trafficking and exploitation. The solution requires an integrated response that depends upon collaboration between law enforcement, academic, non-governmental and corporate actors. However, the use of ICT and the Internet by traffickers for the recruitment and exploitation of children and vulnerable adults is surprisingly under-researched, except perhaps in relation to child sexual abuse and gender-based violence, which has received much more scholarly and political attention and effort.

The European Online Grooming Project (Webster et al, 2012) investigated ICT logistics, conversation management and offending location to develop typologies of offenders and victims. Other studies have developed typologies of online sexual predators, users of child-abuse images, and different patterns of ICT-facilitated sexual abuse and exploitation. While Musto and Boyd identified that there is a widely held recognition that technology functions as both a facilitator and disrupter of human trafficking in general, there is a lack of research that critically investigates how the latter can effectively contribute to anti-trafficking efforts. They found that as technologies grow more sophisticated so too will be the possibilities for developing 'innovative socio-technological interventions; yet capitalising on this knowledge requires far more low-tech solutions; specifically, political will and agitation for redistributive justice' (p 477). Focusing on the online sexual exploitation of children (OSEC) in the Philippines, Fell and Jesperson agreed, arguing that 'online behaviours of children have direct implications on how OSEC can be understood better for deterrence purposes. For example, research specific to Internet and social media technology in relation to OSEC is especially relevant given the "huge transformation in the range and speed of communication" associated with globalisation'[4] (p 62).

Musto and Boyd's criticism of the lack of political will was directed at lawmakers and protective systems and policies in the US, but similar criticism has been levelled at the UK. In their 2022 report for Crest Advisory, Calouri et al (2022) suggest that we have a collective social media blind spot (p 13) concerning the relationship between social media and youth violence. Since 2016, when the UK Government Home Office designated criminal exploitation as a specific category of modern slavery, referrals into the National Referral Mechanism (NRM) have dramatically increased, as have the number of children under the age of 19 being treated in hospital for stab wounds (Calouri et al, 2022). Calouri et al have found in their previous research that 'social media plays a number of instrumental roles in a range of criminal pursuits, especially in the UK's £9.4 billion market for illegal drugs' (Calouri et al, 2022, p 14). In its serious violence strategy, 2018, the UK government Home Office cited evidence that gangs use social media to promote their businesses and criminal activity as well as for the purposes of recruitment.

The prosecutions of traffickers in Operation FORT and Operation PELTIER presented large quantities of evidence adduced from phone data, including text messages, contacts lists, dates, times and duration of telephone calls made to and received from phones registered to offenders and victims.

---

[4]   Citing Stafford et al (2011).

Caroline Haughey KC[5] who prosecuted both cases explained how, in Operation FORT, digital data was vital evidence that illustrated the modus operandi of the OCG.

> This case did not rest exclusively on what was heard from the complainants, often what they say and what has happened to them can be independently verified. A phone number on an employment application form for example may be on the form of a specific complainant but actually be a handset that is in fact attributable to a defendant as it was recovered from their person ... Bank accounts in one complainant's name are often used to receive the wages of another complainant. But those accounts are also used to apply for loans and pay for insurance and when traces on those insurance policies take place they link back to defendants being insured on cars.
>
> Employment records show how much they [victims] earned, banking documents show how little they received and what lack of control they had over their lives.
>
> There was evidence from the DWP [Department of Work and Pensions] about the use of defendant's phone numbers to make calls to claim benefits in the names of complainants, there were applications to utilities companies, there were the recovery of banking documents, bank cards and PIN numbers of complainants at the addresses of defendants, and indeed in their cars and on their person.

In Operation PELTIER, the gang used the Internet to advertise the women that they were controlling for prostitution through adult websites.

> Marika is the half-sister of Katarina. She told Police in Hungary that they were in regular contact on Facebook. One day, in 2013, she received a message

---

[5]   Personal colleague to the author.

from Katarina on Facebook stating that she had been kidnapped by JB. Immediately after this message was sent, another message came saying 'No, you're an idiot'. Marika said that she was very surprised at this as it was totally out of character for Katarina and so she replied 'Your mother's an idiot' – that was the end of that particular conversation.

Marika was concerned that her sister's account had been hacked so contacted her again and asked her questions that only Katarina would know the answers to. Katarina told her that she had escaped and she was now in a good place. She informed Marika that she had told the police and that she would be home soon.

In November 2013 Katarina returned home and went to see her Marika and repeated that she had been kidnapped, by JB and taken to the UK and that she had escaped from an address in London after the other female in the address had fallen asleep. Marika described Katarina as anxious and unhappy. Marika saved the messages, which became a part of the evidence bundle.

After her escape, Katarina described how JB monitored her Facebook account and her online activity. Evidence relating to other women that the group recruited and controlled for prostitution showed how the group utilised social media to contact, recruit and direct girls. Crucially, social media was also used to try and persuade women who had left the group to return.

Degrees of organisation in trafficking of human beings for the purpose of exploitation

Increasingly, trafficked people are being exploited through multiple activities concurrently; for example, criminal exploitation in conjunction with sexual exploitation (Anti-Slavery International, 2014). Obtaining people to exploit is not difficult for OCGs but may vary by region and the type of exploitative activity for which the victim is to be used. Globally, particularly vulnerable groups include: unaccompanied migrant children; people living on the streets and in extreme poverty; people who have had a very low level of education, this with alcoholism and other addictions; victims of domestic violence; refugees displaced by conflict and natural disasters and so on; people from poor, marginalised communities; neglected or abused children; and children who dropped out of school (Surtees, 2005; Ionescu and Fusu-Plaiasu, 2008; Shelley, 2010).

Human trafficking is usually assumed to be found in the nexus of demand, supply and profit. Examples such as Operation GOLF, Operation FORT and Operation JOKER/KRONE show that the profits are substantial to the controller of the victim. However, the controller may in some instances be considered the first-order beneficiary or user of the victim, but there may be a system of second-order beneficiaries who act as facilitators, suppliers of the workers or the suppliers of licit and illicit goods and services who all profit from the criminal activities. Indeed, human trafficking may be the lucrative tip of a criminal iceberg, its earnings funding both criminal and legal activities and creating the opportunity for cooperative activities between criminals.

In other cases, crime may be a characteristic of a family or affiliation group and its members' functioning and therefore compliance with, and participation in, criminal activities may be a normal experience and a condition for remaining within and protected by the family or group. In such a context, a family may constitute an OCG in its own right (though the value of this use of the construct may be debateable).

The degrees of organisation diagram (Figure 3.1) is an illustration of the importance of relationships between the person that is engaged in exploitative activity and the beneficiaries and controllers of that activity. The diagram is a graphic representation of three scenarios in which an exploited individual may be caused to engage in criminal activity.

Scenario 1: The potential victim is enagaging in the activity voluntarily, who gains from the proceeds of their activity is not being subjected to exploitation. The person's motivation is likely to relate to his or her own physical, emotional, psychological and social needs; for example, food, warmth, shelter, safety, security, affiliation, kudos and even as an act of self-actualisation

Figure 3.1: The degrees of organisation

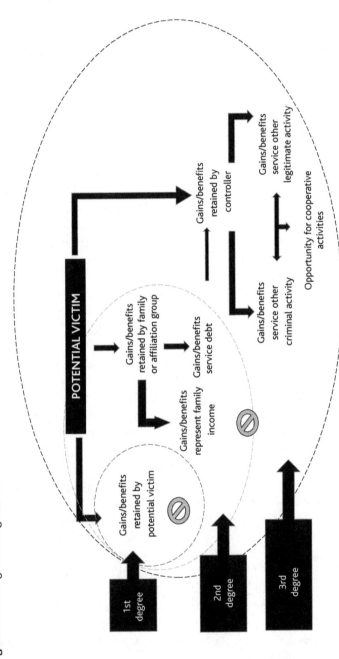

Source: Barlow and Murphy, forthcoming

(Maslow, [1943] 2014). Lower-level needs may be indicative of isolation or social marginalisation, desperation or neglect by informal as well as statutory support services and protective agents. Their problems and behaviour such as engagement in crime or socially unacceptable behaviour may cause them to be marginalised within society and labelled as delinquent while at the same time increasing the their visibility and exposure to other criminals. This may also increase their vulnerability to exploitation by predatory others.

Case example: transcript of short interviews with perpetrator and victim of child criminal exploitation for street drug dealing

Like the recruitment of children for sexual exploitation, recruiters for criminal exploitation target children from poor backgrounds who are already engaged in offending behaviour, children experiencing problems at home or those who are in local authority care. The following brief case study is a transcript of two television interviews. The first interview is with a dealer, 'Paco', who ran a drug deal line (a phone number used to advertise availability and connect with customers to arrange sales). The second interview is with a young person, Chris, who was exploited as a runner, carrying drugs, money and weapons, and selling drugs on the behalf of his criminal controllers. The interviews have been transcribed from a Sky News report (Hirsch, 2015).

'Paco' is a former gang member. He claims to have made thousands of pounds by sending up to ten young people a year into a small town where they were sometimes subject to violent attacks; they are also often subjected to arrest by the police.

Paco: Workers, they range from White, Black, fat, skinny, young, old, whoever wants to work. They're just out there. They're on the estate, trying to get attention by doing little things. They want to be known, want to be with the big guys. You kind of noticed them as well ... You just approach say what; you want to go to the country? He goes yeah, okay. Cool, you start.

Probably went through like ten workers at least because some of them mess up, some are arrested. Some just can't handle the pressure. You gotta sack them so … You just go through them like water.

Hirsch: What happens if they mess up?

Paco: You might just think yeah, I'm going to pocket half the money. Starts messing up, obviously is punishment innit?

Hirsch: And he can get killed for that?

Paco: Can do. He's messing with someone's business innit? So, it's not a game as they say.

Hirsch: Can you describe the demographic of the young people that you would recruit to work for you in the countryside?

Paco: I would say from a broken home. I would say from poverty. Lacking something. He needs that male figure in his life, I think. He wants to be a part of something.

Hirsch also interviewed 'Chris' aged 16. Chris was trafficked all over southern England.

Chris: I sold class A, crack, heroin, in the city as well. We go and stay up there even a crackhead's house or a B&B: I didn't like it. Crackheads can be quite violent sometimes, you know, you've got money and they want to rob you for it. I've got friends who'd been cut on their faces. I've got friends who been hit with needles. So yeah, they can be quite violent, and they want to come. So, there's the potential of that, being apprehended and charged with intent to supply – which can face a lot of years in prison for that, you know?

Regarding young people's choices Chris explains:

Maybe they haven't got the same footing in their estate and they're kind of being exploited because they don't really have a choice. If they want things to run smoother for them in their community, it's better that they go and do this because it might give them some immunity.

While Paco hints at violent punishment, including potentially the killing of a young person who has 'messed up', Chris's account shows that the violence perpetrated against young people in the context of drug dealing is not only from the controllers but also from other exploited people; for example, the people in the trap houses who are both vulnerable and exploited and violent offenders.

Scenario 2: A person that is engaged in work or other activity but hands over the proceeds to their family or affiliates may or may not be subjected to exploitation. The activity may, however, be a part of the family's or group functioning as a system; namely, the family may adhere to anti-social narratives and criminality or otherwise socially unacceptable behaviour is expected or tolerated by the adults, carers and extended family peers. The activity may be indicative of family or group poverty and survival needs, low resiliance and marginalisation. Both the individual and their family or affiliation group are vulnerable to exploitation by predatory others.

Scenario 3: The individual and/or the family or group hand over the proceeds from the activity to another or others. The payment is in respect to services (for example, protection, people smuggling, 'problem-solving') or to service debt to the other(s); for example, loansharks.

Case example: Operation GOLF – Roma family

In his investigation of child exploitation of Roma children in London through begging and benefit fraud, BBC journalist John Sweeney visited Romania and spoke to Roma families. In Romania there are 2 million Roma people living in dire poverty. Sweeney found a Roma village in which the inhabitants were segregated from the rest of Romanian society. The living conditions shown in his film are harsh: none of the adults had regular employment, there is no running water and homes are mere shacks in disrepair. In one of these shacks lived a family of 17 people. Sweeney talked to a man and woman with their son who appears to be about 11 years old.

Father: We have no money. We have nothing. My wife goes begging in the village.

Mother: I'm his mother and if I go begging I'll take him with me because he's more likely to get a bit of bread because he's a child. But they don't give any to me. They say 'Go and work' but they give him a bit of bread.

Sweeney: The kids are taught the technique of how to beg by their mothers.

Mother: And I tell them to say 'Lady have mercey on me. Have charity for the love of God'.

Sweeney: [illustrates the point made by Ballet et al] As the children are the main bread winners, going to school comes second to begging ... If they [adults] borrow money from the Gypsey loan sharks they have to pay back, big time.

He heard from another woman: 'Here, for 100 we have to pay back 200 but what are we going to live on if we have to pay that interest with seven or eight children?'

Sweeney's report supports the report by the European Rights Centre (2011) and Brotherton and Waters (2013) when he explains that, according to police, families become slaves to the gangsters, forced to beg to pay off debt.

This case study is an example of Scenario 2. However, the desperate poverty identified by Sweeney in his television documentary renders famillies vulnerable to the predatory loansharks. Thus the 'degrees of organisation' diagram may be interpreted as representing an aetiological system. Crucially, the family in this situation are already dependent upon begging to gain a sufficient income to survive and, as Mother explains, her son is more likely to receive some form of payment because he is a child; he is better able to generate income preciseiy because he is a child and this value is also recognised by the gangsters. The disquieting fact is that for this family, their children are their only asset, a means of income but for the gangsters the family with its child assets become a suitable target for exploitation: the gangsters may control the parents who in turn control the children or hand the children over in a transaction that ensures the survival needs of the parents and siblings are met.

Understanding the structural complexities of this crime group is only made possible by understanding its activities in the context of the Romanian Roma social history and lived experiences of the people. The case also highlights the uncomfortable issue of an exploited person's participation in the abuse and exploitation of others; that is, vulnerable adults in this context are targeted and recruited for exploitation. In turn, they target and recruit even more vulnerable people, such as their own children or other child family members.

The degrees of organisation diagram (Figure 3.1) is an illustration of the importance of relationships between the individual that is being caused to engage in some form of work or other activity and the beneficiaries and controllers of that activity. The diagram is a graphic representation of three scenarios, which require different degrees of organisation according to the goals of the person or group that are controlling the activity.

The exploitation may therefore constitute organised crime if it is accepted that, as Cressey (1969) suggests, the criminal activity requires some degree of organisation. If crime is a part of the family's or group functioning, the organisation is the family or group system but a family or group that forces some of its members to engage in certain activities, such as commit crime, beg or sex work, may be coerced to do so by a stronger, controlling crime group.

Conclusion

Trafficking and modern slavery and other forms of exploitation emerge from complex systems that have a dynamic functional relationship. Each of these systems act as elements of the exploitation system and can be defined and described separately as the victim system, perpetrator system and environment system.

The exploitation system can exist only at the intersection of the other three but will vary depending upon the configuration of the other elements and their relationships with each other.

The investigation and prosecution of human trafficking offences includes many examples of the multiple and mixed ways in which individual victims are exploited by traffickers, some of which are included in this book. Elsewhere I have described other cases that have concerned victims who have escaped their traffickers only to be re-trafficked by those who offered to help them (Barlow and Murphy, forthcoming).

Slavery, servitude, forced labour, sexual exploitation and forced criminality are an output or product of the exploitation process. The nature of exploitation is largely immaterial to understanding trafficking and slavery as it is the process and mechanisms that are important. The mechanisms of exploitation are the abuse of the position of vulnerability, including physical abuse, emotional and psychological abuse, sexual abuse and neglect. These are all forms of maltreatment without which exploitation cannot occur. Understanding the phenomenon of human trafficking and modern slavery, therefore, requires a 'bottom-up' approach that starts from recognising a pattern of abusive behaviour and relationships.

Abuse, coercive control and neglect occurs in the context of a relationship in which there is a substantial imbalance of power that is misused by the stronger person to control and harm the weaker for some form of gain (to satisfy a need, objective or overall aim). The nature and extent of the abuse together with the degree of harm will vary according to:

- the needs, objectives and aims of the perpetrator(s);
- the characteristics of the victim and what these represent to the perpetrator(s); and
- the environments which the victim and perpetrators share and in which the abuse occurs.

A systemic theoretical model that seeks to describe and explain human trafficking and modern slavery must be a synthesis of theories that have proven useful in the fields of criminology and safeguarding and public protection, as well as social and behavioural psychology.

4

Trafficking and modern slavery: complex patterns of exploitation

The previous chapter demonstrated how trafficking, modern slavery, exploitation and organised crime have all presented academics, professionals, policy makers and lawmakers with constant definitional challenges. As Haughey (2016b) points out, it is hard to say precisely what constitutes a threshold for exploitation or what evidence might be used to identify its presence, but we tend to know it when we see it. This, it seems, goes to the heart of the problem that is encountered when trying to define the problem in order to legislate for it and develop policies and regulatory frameworks. All the laudable efforts of academics, legislators and policy makers that were discussed in that chapter describe the phenomenon but lack explanatory power for why and how it occurs and is concentrated upon particular populations or groups, in different places over time. To solve this problem requires theory. Theory explains a phenomenon, why and how it occurs or does not occur. Theory provides a foundation and logic for the development of approaches for responding to the phenomenon, preventing or mitigating it. Theory can be quantified, tested and developed so that approaches can be strengthened, refined and adapted to changing conditions.

In this chapter, I argue that these definitional problems occur because there is a tendency to try to define a problem and work backwards to identify correlates and causes in a linear pathway of logic – if A then B. Trafficking does not follow neat linear causal pathways – it is complex and non-linear. Human trafficking and exploitation is a complex pattern of transactions that emerges from the synergistic, dynamic relationships between the exploiters and the exploited (Barlow et al, 2021; Green, Heys, and Barlow, forthcoming). It is a social phenomenon.

Theories of complexity

The application of complex systems theory to a social phenomenon such as trafficking and modern slavery provides a theoretical foundation for its analysis as a pattern that emerges from social interactions that are autonomous and non-linear; the relationships self-organise according to a small number of relatively simple rules that are accepted based upon shared purpose and cultural norms (Gelfland et al, 2011).

According to complexity theory, a system is built upon structures that self-organise by interacting with their environments. They are flexible and adaptive in changing circumstances and can transform small-scale (micro-state) irregularities into large-scale (macro-state) patterns. This makes them robust and resilient over time (Hassett and Stevens, 2014).

A human being is one complex system, which exists within wider complex systems (family, friendships, communities, society). Every person, as a component of a social system, has their own motivations and needs which will drive them towards perceived opportunities to meet those needs (Maslow, [1943] 2014). Other individuals or groups that have synergistic needs and motivations will endeavour to attract them to join. When we label something as exploitation, we may therefore refer to patterns of complex behaviour that emerge from relatively simple local interactions between system components over time (Manson, 2001).

Who comes to be exploited by whom, how, when and where depends upon a multitude of factors: their relationships with and to each other; their current state of development and social capital; the knowledge, experience and beliefs that inform their decisions; and the terms of the relationship. Each person, let's call them actors, has their own needs or goals. To meet those needs or goals, each actor is largely reliant upon their respective knowledge and experience of the social, cultural, political, economic and geographical environment in which they exist.

I argue here for the need to understand exploitation first and foremost as a pattern of abusive behaviour that has particular goals. By doing so, it is possible to draw upon vast knowledge in professional and academic literature and upon clinical experience. On this basis, it is possible to apply extant knowledge about the social and psychological processes of abuse, coercion and control and victim impact, perpetrator motivation and behaviour. Reframing the understanding of cases of human trafficking and modern slavery as cases of abuse and interpersonal violence or maltreatment through which profit or other gain is generated can offer greater opportunity for flexible, multi-systemic interventions. In some of the case studies, such as D in Operation RASTRELLI who I introduced in the previous chapter, within this chapter, the victims have made choices and taken decisions, which superficially appear to be reckless, dangerous and even collusive with the offenders. A closer analysis reveals that these decisions and choices are rational given the conditions under which they were made and are consistent with choices, decisions and behaviours exhibited by people within other high-stress contexts for abuse and neglect.

The emergence of patterns of exploitation

As noted, patterns of exploitation emerge from the interaction between the victim, the perpetrator and the environment in which both operate over time (Barlow, 2019; Barlow et al, 2021; Barlow and Murphy, forthcoming; Green, Heys, and Barlow, forthcoming).

The concept of emergence is important. A pattern becomes identifiable because it represents a formation of collective behaviours. Put simply, we are identifying what parts of a system do together that they do not do when they are alone. Collective behaviours result from relationships between actors. These relationships are constructed and negotiated based upon a shared purpose and cultural values. These shared goals and values provide the template for individuals to interact with each other, forming and moving between hierarchical groups, which evolve as complex systems. These systems may be national, or even international in scope, but the subsystems and components are never at the same stage of development (Fuller and Myers, 1941). Subsystems and their component parts are limited to local interactions so that in the context of trafficking, victims and perpetrators share a social space, and their interactions reflect a certain level of shared knowledge, local experience, cultural norms and expectations.

Every person as a component of a social system has their own motivations and needs. The motivations and needs act as goals. An individual is likely to be drawn towards conditions, relationships and resources, which might represent opportunities to achieve those goals. Other individuals, groups, communities and institutions may have synergetic needs and motivations. The individual, therefore, represents a potential asset, a resource or an opportunity to assist in the achievement of their own goals. They may then endeavour to attract that person to join them based upon the potential for mutual welfare and benefit. In this situation, both parties are evaluating each other before proceeding to negotiate the transactions and develop the necessary relationship to meet both their shared and separate goals.

The fact that needs and motivations are synergetic does not mean that the relationships between people and groups that make up the system are equal or equitable (Barlow et al, 2021). The complexity of the relationships and interactions between people within a system, therefore, means that it is not possible to characterise the whole system as having a single unifying shared purpose (Manson, 2001). When the power to control information, resources and freedom is weighed against one party in favour of another, the goals of the former may pertain to the maintenance and maximisation of that power and control. This is the foundation of the abuse of the position of vulnerability. The party without that power and control is dependent on the other if they are to have access to any of the information and resources that they need to achieve their motivational goals. These motivating goals reflect what Maslow described as the hierarchy of needs (Maslow, [1943] 2014), such as basic survival needs of food, health care, shelter and safety, as well as social inclusion and advancement.

A person who is trafficked for the purpose of financial or material gain achieved by his/her exploitation must be found and recruited from somewhere; the provider or recruiter of the

Figure 4.1: Three complex systems as the Circles of Analysis: suitable target, motivated perpetrator and conducive environment

victim may be the first party to gain from the exploitation and may be a friend, intimate partner or family member, corrupt officials or others within the victim's community, who, as discussed previously, may meet in everyday settings. In the case of exploitation by family members, the offenders, controllers and end users may all be one and the same (see Figure 4.1).

Winding and branched pathways to exploitation

Patterns of trafficking emerge from interactions between three complex systems: the potential victim that is a *suitable target* for abuse and exploitation, the *motivated perpetrator* of abuse and exploitation and the *environment* in which both the person and perpetrator exists that is *conducive* to the emergence of a pattern of harm.

The suitable target

A person that is a suitable target for exploitation will possess a range of characteristics that will increase their vulnerability to different types of exploiter and exploitation in different contexts.

VALUE:	The suitable target will represent some form of value to the perpetrator. This value depends entirely on the needs and motivations that drive the perpetrator's behaviour.
INERTIA:	This refers to the ease with which suitable target may be controlled by a perpetrator.

	This may be shaped by the nature of the relationship, the target's dependence on the perpetrator and the imbalance of power and dominance within the relationship.
VISIBILITY:	This may be a moot point if the suitable target is being abused or exploited by a family member but is important in terms of understanding how a potential victim comes to the attention of an extra-familial perpetrator. This may be through the suitable target's own behaviour (for example, anti-social behaviour, online activity, the potential victim approaching the perpetrator), their physical characteristics and marginalisation or isolation.
ACCESSIBILITY:	How easily can a suitable target and perpetrator encounter each other. This characteristic relates to the potential victim's relationship with their environment as much as with the potential perpetrator. (Felson and Cohen, 1980; Barlow, 2017, 2019)

Motivated perpetrator

The vulnerability of a potential victim does not indicate that they are destined to be trafficked and exploited. For this to occur, they must be in proximity to a motivated perpetrator, as illustrated in Figure 4.2.

Although a strong motivating factor for trafficking of human beings (THB) in most contexts is financial and material gain (according to the United Nations Office on Drugs and Crime [UNODC], Europol and Interpol, THB is more profitable than drugs and arms trafficking), there is no single motivating factor for a person to become involved as a perpetrator or facilitator of human trafficking, modern slavery or any other form of exploitation. It is multi-factorial and may broadly be said to comprise of the perpetrator's emotional needs, deficits in self-regulation and ability to form or maintain appropriate and healthy relationships (both intra-familial and extra-familial relationships).

Figure 4.2: The Circles of Analysis: interaction between two complex systems – suitable target and motivated perpetrator

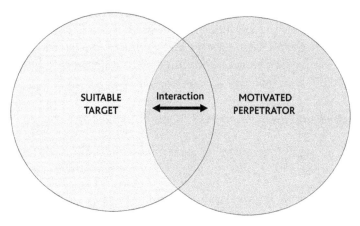

Trafficking and modern slavery is not a single offence crime and people can be repeatedly victimised over time by the same perpetrators or re-victimised at some stage by the same or different perpetrators. Heys (2023) offers a detailed analysis of how historic and current social structures in different contexts create vulnerabilities by constraining choices and, therefore, decision-making, and action, for some individuals and groups while creating opportunities for exploitation by dominant individuals and groups. People that have been found to be victims of trafficking and exploitation have often been victimised from a younger age and over several years (Murphy et al, 2022).

Exploitation often emerges from the following sequence of interaction between victims and perpetrators: ensnaring, creating dependency, taking control and finally total dominance. This will likely be familiar to many who have addressed the issue of domestic abuse, intimate partner violence and stalking and other contexts for coercive and controlling relationships.

In this section I examine how these interactions can be seen to lead to different patterns of exploitation with reference to three case studies.

Ensnaring

Many victims of human trafficking intend to travel while comparatively few are abducted. However, it is very common for people to be enticed to travel by the promise of good employment, high earnings and accommodation, constituting the first pillar of the trafficking offence ('actions').

Case example: Operation FORT – 'Job in England immediately'

Szymon arrived in England on 9 January 2015. He came to the UK because of an advertisement with an offer of work, which he had seen in a shop. The content of the advertisement was as follows – 'Job in England immediately'. The advertisement contained also a Polish mobile number with no further particulars. Szymon called the number to obtain more details. He was told by the Polish man that answered that there was a packing job available in England and that he could go there straight away and that he should gather as many friends as possible because there was lots of work. He was also told how they would get there and that travelling costs would be gradually deducted from their earnings when they had started working. The same would apply to the food – it would be provided and then cost deducted from earnings. He was told he would be earning 300 pounds a week for a packing job from which 20 pounds would be deducted weekly for the accommodation but he was not told the amount that would be deducted for the travel and food that was to be provided.

Agata is a Polish woman who arrived in England in November 2014. She was recruited like others in Poland, on this occasion receiving a call from one of her friends who informed her of an advert for a job where the wages were £140 a week and there would be help with accommodation and food with free transport there.

Agata and her partner Filip called the number from the advert and spoke to a man who gave the name 'Andrzej'. He confirmed the contents of the advert and invited them to meet him at his address. Agata and Filip went to Andrzej's address and found a number of other people there all going to various locations in the UK. Agata and Filip travelled by minibus together with nine other people and arrived in the UK in November 2014.

Case example: Operation PELTIER – 'The Lover Boy'

Katarina had been trafficked to the UK for the purposes of sexual exploitation through forced prostitution. She seized an opportunity to escape from the house in which she was being held and found her way to a police station. During her interview she told specially trained police officers she was born in 1989 and was brought up by the state in an institution. At the age of 18 she moved back with her father before having a child with an older man.

Still pregnant, she then entered what she believed was to be a romantic relationship with JB. It was he that made her work as a prostitute. She described a violent relationship in which JB threatened to kill her every time she left him to return to her family. Her child was born and subsequently was taken into state care.

Case example: Suhail Alim and Zulaiha – married into servitude

Suhail Alim married Zulaiha, a young woman from Pakistan, by way of arrangement in Pakistan on 25 June 2006. Zulaiha did not initially come to the UK with Suhail as she wished to complete her degree in Islamic studies in Pakistan and there was some delay in getting her visa arranged. They continued to see each other when Suhail returned to Pakistan, but the marriage was not consummated. The families were known to each other, and the marriage was by mutual arrangement and agreement.

In 2007 she applied for her spousal visa which was refused but eventually was granted in December 2012.

Zulaiha subsequently arrived in the UK a few days later and lived with her husband and her mother-in-law in their four-bedroom house. She was a well-educated and skilled woman and she expected to be entering a harmonious household where she would be treated equally. Having only completed the Nikah Ceremony it was tradition that the marriage was not consummated until *Valeema* (wedding party), which took place after her arrival in England.

The *Valeema* subsequently took place in early 2013; however, even then the marriage was not consummated and, in fact, never was. It became clear to her that the purpose of the marriage was neither a traditional one, nor an equal one, but rather in the words of Suhail – he had married her so she could look after his mother and his house. This was no mutually desired match based on friendship or love but rather she was a convenient servant to work within the household and tend to the needs of the family. If those needs were not met then she was subjected to aggression, violence and bullying.

Creating dependency

The trafficker may induce emotional dependency in the victim as a means (the second pillar of the trafficking offence), offering them love, affection, affiliation, encouragement, affirmation and then also having the ability to withdraw all of these when the victim is non-compliant, has failed in some way or simply to encourage them to do more. Sometimes the dependency may relate to the perception of protection of the trafficker or creating substance dependence.

Case example: Suhail and Zulaiha Alim

The *Valeema* having taken place there was an expectation by Zulaiha that the wedding would be consummated – each and every time she enquired of Suhail if this would happen, he would react in an aggressive manner.

The first specific incident of violence she recalls was when she asked her husband for sex when they were in the bedroom – his reaction was to slap her twice across the face, pull her hair and push her. He called her 'a whore, a bitch, and a shameless person'. This was one of the first of many aggressive, violent and degrading reactions to her any time her Suhail considered that she not to do as directed and to have shown 'disrespect'.

Any request or indeed mention of sex to her husband resulted in him assaulting her. One evening, having completed her night prayer Zulaiha again spoke to Suhail about sex – he picked up a lamp from the table and hit her on the head, threw a glass of water at her and then hit her with the water bottle.

Zulaiha was too terrified to discuss the matter with anyone as she had been told that if she spoke to anyone about her domestic problems the family would kill her. Her existence was one of controlled isolation within a rigid frame of rules. The Court heard how her sole purpose was to answer the needs of her husband and mother-in-law as an unpaid servant who was treated with contempt and violence.

Suhail Alim was described by Prosecutor Caroline Haughey KC as a bully, who enjoyed deploying control over her. He deprived her of any money – giving her only £10 per month with which to keep in contact with her family. Beyond that she had little to nothing. She was told that all she needed was in the house and when she accompanied her mother-in-law, she was told she was not allowed to purchase anything as she was told she should not waste her husband's money. If taken shopping it was only for the purposes of carrying the bags. She was responsible for the cooking, cleaning, gardening, washing and ironing.

Case example: Operation PELTIER – Katarina

After her child was born, she described being sent to Austria by JB to work and JB refusing to let her return to her family, she was able to contact her local authority on the Internet and made a complaint of being kept prisoner. She recalled that the Local Authority notified the police, and a search warrant was issued for her.

She returned home having received the message about the warrant and JB together with some of his friends took her to the police station. In fact, it was JB who had told her she needed to return home to deal with the warrant. She described telling the police what had happened but was very frightened and so was unable to tell the police that the people who had kept her captive were the very people who had taken her to the police station.

She left with JB, and having spent some time with her parents and described getting back together with JB who made her work on the street as a prostitute and took all her money from this work. Such was his influence over her and her dependence upon him, that despite the opportunity to move away, she repeatedly returned to him.

There was a brief period when she lived with another male who was helping her; however, she returned to JB who had contacted her on Facebook declaring his love to her. He persuaded her to steal money from her former partner and return to him – some few days later he purchased a ticket for her and they flew to London.

When JB had asked her to come and work with him as a prostitute, he had demanded her answer quickly as there were other girls who were going to work in England too. She described a relationship based on fear: he had assaulted her by putting his hand around her throat, which frightened her. He also told her that he would protect her when she was working as a prostitute in England.

Taking control

The perpetrator will increasingly isolate the target from their usual support networks, use increasingly coercive techniques, including subtle ones, which may be a combination of psychological and physical. The perpetrator will increasingly control the victim's money, resources and movements – even when they eat, sleep and use the bathroom.

Jesperson and Henriksen (2023) point out that a particular challenge faced by traffickers and perpetrators of modern slavery is the risk that their victims may escape and, if they do so, inform the authorities. Various means of control may be combined to not only ensure compliance with their instructions and demands but also to prevent victims from even considering escape. Furthermore, even if they do escape, the fear and anxiety that has been cultivated during the exploitation may ensure that a victim is more likely to return to them. These control strategies combine physical abuse, sexual abuse, psychological and emotional abuse, and may include confiscation of identity or any other important documents (residence permit card, insurance, car, labour contract, birth certificate and so on), withholding of money, food and other essentials, isolation and even renaming victims.

Case example: Operation FORT

Agata and her partner Filip went by minibus together with nine other people and arrived in the UK in late November 2014. They were taken to an address in Dudley, near Birmingham, England. Upon their arrival a man came out of the house and paid £160 for her and Filip's travel. When Agata got into the house, she was introduced to a man called Dominik who immediately told them that they owed him £300–£400 for their transport as well as the other items such as a mattress and so on.

Dominik then took them to another address in Dudley where they were shown to a room upstairs. There was no heating in the room and the walls were covered in damp – the property had no hot water.

The following Monday Dominik took them to a high-street bank where he acted as their interpreter. He told them to provide the bank with a different address to the one at which they were staying but rather to give his (Dominik's) address in Dudley. He also informed them that he would be keeping their bankcard and would then be the one who gave them their money which he would be splitting from their earnings.

Agata and Filip remained at the address for a week and despite asking for matters to improve Dominik told that them that he needed time.

Having obtained the bankcard, the couple where then registered with an employment agency in Leicester who gave them work at a waste recycling centre in Walsall. The job was very demanding and exhausting but Agata was told by Dominik she had to work overtime to earn more money. He asked her to work a 7-day week, which she refused, and so he sent his stepfather Ryszard Brzezinski to intimidate her by shouting abuse at her.

This continued until 11 February 2015. Dominik would attend on a Friday to provide their earnings, which despite being £360 Agata would be given £100, the remainder having been deducted by him for fictional expenses. Filip recalled Dominik saying that his weekly wage was £300, but that he needed to give Dominik £150 and then a further £70 for transport and accommodation. This left him with only £80.

Case example: Suhail and Zuhaila Alim

As tradition dictates Zuhaila came to the marital home with wedding jewellery – this was taken off her and kept from her. Despite her asking for its return on a number of occasions she was told that if she wore it then people would kill her and snatch it from her.

Although some of this jewellery was returned in due course to the police, Zuhaila described items still missing as including a small necklace, two pairs of earrings and one ring. This was another means of exploiting and controlling her, depriving her of her personal belongings and particularly the jewellery resulted in her absolute financial dependence on her husband and his family.

Zuhaila was not allowed out unaccompanied and, when she was alone at home, she was rung every ten minutes to make sure the phone was not engaged and her movements both within and outside the house were monitored by other members of the family. Suhail Alim combined physical and emotional abuse to coerce and control his wife but also rationalised this with a distortion of social, religious and cultural norms that his wife had grown up with. She had grown up in a stable, loving and nurturing environment that supported her academic and professional aspirations alongside which it was her expectation and belief that she would be a good wife and willingly fulfil many traditional, gendered duties associated with being a wife and daughter-in-law. Suhail's assertion that all husbands hit their wives and the treatment of her as an unpaid servant were grotesque distortions of her own values and traditions.

Jesperson and Henriksen (2023, p34) describe how, in other contexts, traffickers have made use of juju rituals in Nigeria to control women and girls.

> During the ritual the girls' hair or fingernails are taken and they swear an oath to a deity. This process binds the girl to the contract to repay her debt for transportation. Girls are genuinely scared of the ritual and believe they will be plagued by nightmares or go crazy if they do not fulfil their obligation.

The use of juju manipulates culturally specific conventions to control girls in order to minimise the need for direct oversight. The girls instead self-discipline as they are indirectly controlled by their fear of juju. This is particularly useful when they are working on the street and direct control is not possible.

Case example: Operation PELTIER – Katarina

JB bought a SIM card for Katarina's phone and took it from her and began to use it in England.

Upon her arrival in Peterborough through JB she got to know Zsolt. She was collected from the airport by a woman she knew as Szilvia who had been sent to collect her by Zsolt (Szilvia was said to be the daughter of Erno) and it was she who drove them to Peterborough. JB drove the car while he and Szilvia discussed how they conducted the brothel business; how many girls worked for them, how much money would have to be paid and so on. Katarina was asked by Szilvia whether she had a passport and, if so, it would be easier to create the profiles and delete them every three days. She was also asked by Szilvia whether she had any sexy images of herself and when she said no Szilvia informed her that some would have to be taken. She was also told that she would have to learn relevant English phrases so that she could be sold to the clients.

She was taken to an address in Peterborough. There were two other girls at the address – Hanna (who she later worked with) and Csilla whom she knew from Hungary.

JB informed her he would be buying her suitable clothing for her work but that she would have to earn some money to cover the cost. She got dressed and Hanna and Szilvia took photos of her and put them on the website. She explained how she had to take up various poses and remove items of clothing as directed by Szilvia – she did not feel she had any choice.

She asked Szilvia if she would have to work that day and was told that since no profile had been created, she could rest. Having been shown her room in the house Katarina recalled going down to the kitchen and a conversation between JB and Zslot who showed a pack of money that had been earned by Hanna. JB said to Katarina that they would be able to return to Hungary more quickly if she could earn as well as Hanna.

In the brothel, Szilvia would act as the receptionist sending the clients in and allowing them to choose a girl. The service would be paid for and after the client had finished, the money was taken straight down to either Hanna, or Csilla or JB if he was present. Katarina was not permitted to keep any of her money save small amounts to buy cigarettes and so on. She also recalls that EM collected the money and was responsible for arranging the rental of the properties.

Katarina remained in the UK on this occasion for about three weeks before returning to Hungary, being kept at a friend of JB's house and then returning with JB to England. She describes her return journey to Hungary the first time as being with a male called Csabi who drove and dropped her and JB at a railway station in Budapest where they were met by members of JB's family. She stayed with them for a few days and was accompanied every time she left the house.

She returned to Peterborough some weeks later with JB and two other people, Dezso and Evi. She carried on working as a prostitute and was frequently returned to Hungary by car again with Csabi driving.

Total dominance

This is achieved when the perpetrator controls every aspect of the victim's life to the extent that they do not even have to be present. The victim may be both terrified of the perpetrator but simultaneously dependent upon them which leads to a paradoxical attachment to the perpetrator (Cantor and Price, 2007; van der Watt and van der Westhuizen, 2017).

Case example: Operation FORT

Over a period of approximately two weeks Agata and Filip managed to pay Dominik off and told him that they wished to be independent, and they would be looking to work somewhere else. Agata told Dominik that she was pregnant. Dominik told the couple that he was going to introduce them to his cousin Adam as he had 30 people working for him and that he would pay them on time.

Two days later Adam arrived at the house and indicated that Agata and Filip would be working for him. On 11 February they were moved to yet another address, this time in Walsall. Although there was heating and hot water they had to sleep on the floor as Adam refused to provide them with a mattress.

They continued to work at the recycling centre, and they received half of their wage from Adam, thereafter he refused to pay them. He also kept Filip's ID card.

Filip was then offered a job in Kidderminster. That job only lasted for about a week, and he was then laid off. Agata and Filip were expecting Adam to come to the house on this date – he arrived in a very angry state and told Filip that he was going to fine him £5,000 and that he would 'make him a drug addict and he would be working as a male prostitute in order to pay that debt off'.

Adam also intimidated Agata by making implicit threats about her family in Poland. He gave them both a fake bank account and told Agata to use this for her work. She worked for a week and Adam too began to take half of her earnings, and at the beginning of April Adam moved them to another address in Walsall.

Case example: Suhail and Zuhaila Alim

One evening, on returning home from work, Suhail was told by his mother that she was not satisfied with the standard of care Zuhaila had been providing to her. When he returned home from work, he was furious with his wife and suddenly 'started punching, slapping and kicking' her. He was swearing at her and told her that if his mother asked her to stand in the heavy rain that is what she should do, or indeed stand on one leg.

On another occasion he lost his temper with Zuhaila, hitting her across the head with a wooden board and pulling her hair. He kept telling her 'All husbands hit their wives. Families stay intact because of the sacrifices of women, just tolerate everything.' Despite being covered in bruises Zuhaila was not allowed to see a doctor.

Any attempt at notional independence or perceived disrespect of her husband, his mother or the family was met with direct violence by Suhail. Zuhaila described how, when applying for her national insurance number and having asked her husband for help, he became angry and grabbed her by the throat and smothered her with a cushion with his left hand. She forced him off and ran downstairs. It was a catalogue of abuse culminating in the police being called by neighbours.

It was mid-February 2014 when police were called to the family address, not by Zuhaila, for she did not have free access to her mobile phone, nor any phone. She reported, at the time, being hit and beaten by hand and bottle by her husband – he hit her on the back and head and punched her in the face pushing her on the bed and in her face. Terrified by his behaviour towards her, Zuhaila had begged Suhail to stop and ran from the house screaming.

She was dragged back to the house by Suhail and her mother-in-law, the latter part of this having been seen by a couple of neighbours – two young women who shared a flat.

Suhail's mother assured the police that there was not any incident of concern and due to fear of and intimidation by her husband's family Zuhaila withdrew her allegation. She was told by Suhail to lock herself in her bedroom and then while the police were at the address told by her mother-in-law to go and hide herself in the garden shed. Barefooted, she crossed the back garden to hide in the wooden shed as she had been told.

Having believed that the police had left she came out of the shed only to be seen by the attending officers who asked her to sit in their car – Zuhaila was asked her name and address and having initially given them a different address she told them where she lived. The police subsequently arrested Suhail.

Suhail was hostile towards the police officer and initially refused him entry into the house. He said that his wife was no longer there and there was nothing to be concerned about, that it was a family argument and would be resolved in a few days.

As the officer returned to the police car, he came across Zuhaila and could see injuries to her face particularly to her eye – she was barefoot, not wearing a coat and was wearing only a dress. She was reluctant to give her name and said that she had fallen over which was how she was injured. The officer and his colleague returned to the house to arrest Suhail while one of his brothers spoke to Zuhaila and took her to stay at his home.

When Suhail was cautioned by the officers on his arrest for assault and actual bodily harm, his response was 'Is she making charges, did she say I hit her?'

Zuhaila was now at her brother-in-law's home where he shouted and swore at Zuhaila, throwing a glass of water at her. On 18 February, when the police came to see Zuhaila again, she signed a document agreeing that her husband should be released and that she was not under any pressure.

Case example: Operation PELTIER

One morning, while she was back in Hungary with Csabi, JB and his family, Katarina left the house to buy some cigarettes and came across her former boyfriend. She got into his car and chatted, she became upset and then she received a call from JB. He asked her why she was crying (being able to hear it in her voice over the phone); she returned to the house and JB arrived about an hour later and demanded her former boyfriend's number. JB then called him and threatened him with violence.

Katarina managed to return to Hungary in August to her family home until she was kidnapped by JB. She described him requesting her ID documents and then taking her to Zsolt's house as he wanted to do something. She and JB entered the house then left with Zsolt. They went to another address and then JB drove her to yet another place. She asked to return home and he refused and said that they were going to the UK – he told her she could either go to the UK or he would take her to a remote place and beat her and do the same to her family. Katarina had no choice and so she agreed but repeatedly told JB that she no longer wished to be with him.

They returned to Zsolt's address and it was made clear to Katarina she had to do as directed by Zsolt. JB told Zsolt to beat her up if she did not do as she was told. She was taken to a train station and had neither her phone nor her documents; Zsolt bought the ticket for the train and they took the train to Budapest. She recalls JB changing money at the station – the money being what she had made through the sex work. She was then kept at a house of Zsolt that was in Budapest where she was not allowed to leave the building unless she was accompanied; even her Facebook activity was monitored with Zsolt watching her contact with her sister, Malika. She described sending a message to her sister when Zsolt was distracted, telling her that she had been kidnapped. JB, however, read the message and notified Zsolt, and told her if she sent such messages he would kill her family.

Some 3–4 days later a car with two males in it took Katarina and Zsolt to England. She became aware that one of them was called Erno and recognised him as Szilvia's father and who had come to the house in Peterborough. They came to the UK by Ferry. Erno had collected everyone's passports and ID and presented them on their entry. They returned her passport and ID card but she was too frightened to ask for help. She was then taken to the house in London from which she later escaped.

While at the London address photos were taken of her and put on two or three websites through which clients would come to her and to Hanna at the address. The photos were taken by Zsolt and she was made to wear what she described as a see-through nightie.

The website would work with the customer calling a phone number and speaking to the receptionist who spoke English. Details would be discussed and the customer sent to the girl. The customer would attend and monies would be paid to Hanna who then passed them on to Zsolt.

Katarina told Zsolt that she did not want to work as a prostitute. He told her that JB had huge debts and that she had to work off this debt. She asked if she could work off the debt as soon as possible and he told her she would not be going home anytime soon and that in the long term he wanted her to work for him and he would keep some of the money. She described Zsolt as violent and intimidating and had seen him assault Hanna on several occasions at the Peterborough address.

After she had escaped, Katarina was asked during her police interview to describe her relationship with JB. She confirmed it had been an intimate relationship and she believed that he loved her and said that she considered him her partner.

Detective Superintendent Phil Brewer, now retired, headed Operation PELTIER. He explained to me how it had been difficult to establish the structure and network of offenders who exploited Katarina and other women because they were not a specific organised crime group (OCG), as in Operation FORT. They were a looser network of smaller groups or partnerships, all engaged in running brothels, controlling women for prostitution and other offences. Many of the girls working in the brothels that were being run by these people were apparently agreeing to enter the sex industry even though the criminals took as much as half of their earnings. They were still guilty, under British law, of the offence of trafficking for the purposes of sexual exploitation but many of the young women did not identify themselves as being victims in that context. Some of the women had also transitioned into roles in which they recruited other young women or assisted in the exploitation and control of women such as Katarina.

Conclusion

Understanding among the public and many professionals and policy makers of trafficking and modern slavery is often based upon false assumptions about victims, perpetrators, and the processes and manifestations of trafficking and modern slavery. By examining how different patterns of abuse emerge from the interactions between victims and perpetrators within different contexts we can overcome the problem of definition and working back from that definition to plot linear, causal pathways (what may be described as a top-down approach to addressing the problem). Understanding trafficking and modern slavery as emergent patterns of exploitation addresses the non-linear complexity of the problem, allowing us to anticipate and take account of how these patterns adapt and fluctuate over time and in response to changing conditions.

The three case studies presented in this chapter demonstrate the complexity of trafficking and modern slavery. Unlike crimes such as murder, rape or theft, it is not a single event that happens in a specific place, at a particular time under a set of circumstances (van der Watt and van der Westhuizen, 2017), the line between victims and perpetrators is not always clear and the exploited victim can transition between both roles. When victims of trafficking do not reflect what Nils Christie (1986) has termed 'the ideal victim', or whether the victim is perceived to have something to gain, the status of 'victim' becomes less clear (Jesperson and Henriksen, 2023).

Recent attempts to describe human trafficking and modern slavery offences have tended to compound these assumptions through a phenomenological approach to the analysis of the problem, based upon empirical data to generate descriptive typologies. Such typologies have, at their core, an assumption of linear causality suggesting the trafficking and exploitation can be predicted and that such predictions can therefore inform tactical and strategic responses. This is a traditional approach to policing and crime prevention (van der Watt and van der Westhuizen, 2017) that is replicated in approaches to public protection and safeguarding of children and vulnerable adults. This model may have merit in framing the understanding of single-event crimes, to which I have referred, because while the commission of such crimes can be sophisticated and complicated, they essentially comprise an event that has occurred in a particular context at a specific time with an identifiable and comprehensible process. There is an identifiable victim or complainant, the perpetrator, a crime scene and maybe some witnesses to the event. Investigative processes can systematically compile information and evidence that leads towards, or away from, a suspect, the apprehension of the suspect, the prosecution, conviction and sentence (van der Watt and van der Westhuizen, 2017) which results in a clear, linear, cause-and-effect narrative of a crime or set of crimes.

Trafficking and modern slavery are by contrast extremely difficult to detect, understand and combat. As van der Watt and van der Westhuizen (2017) argue, trafficking must be understood from a non-linear, complex-systems perspective to enhance strategic and tactical responses because understanding the complexity means understanding the interrelationships of the phenomenon.

The aetiology of trafficking and modern slavery is a product of interacting systems, the relationships between which influence who will be exploited, how they will be exploited and by whom. The poly-victimisation of some victims that have been exploited may not be an experience that is shared by others that have been exploited (for example, when comparing the stories of Katarina, Zuhaila, Agata and Filip or Szymon). The processes of recruitment control and maintenance of the enterprise will also vary according to the characteristics of the victim, the motivations of the individual exploiters and groups of exploiters and the context in which the exploitation takes place.

Trafficking and modern slavery is one output of complex systems that are comprised of multiple elements, each of which interact with each other and react to the external influences of their environment. There are, therefore, too few fixed variables to develop a reliable, useful typology of trafficking and modern slavery, perpetrator or victim, because the phenomenon is too broad to define succinctly. While this means that the investigation of perpetrators and the identification and safeguarding of victims is a formidable task, understanding human trafficking as an emergent pattern of behaviour should prompt us to look for patterns rather than individual actors and facilitators. Complex adaptive systems are autonomous but self-organise around simple sets of rules which may result in a multitude of different patterns (domestic servitude, forced labour, organ harvesting, sexual exploitation, forced criminality), but such patterns will only emerge if suitable targets for exploitation interact with motivated perpetrators of exploitation within an environment that is conducive to that pattern of exploitation emerging and being sustained over time.

Trafficking, and the resultant harm, is a pattern of behaviour and interactions (Stevens and Hassett, 2007; Hassett and Stevens, 2014; Barlow, 2019). It emerges from the complex interactions of these three existing systems. Each system is comprised of their own elements or characteristics. There is no central control – the exploitation pattern and degree of harm is an output of a series of self-organising interactions between each of the systems (labelled 1, 2 and 3 as follows and illustrated in Figure 4.3).

(1) Suitable target–conducive environment interaction.
(2) Motivated perpetrator–conducive environment interaction.
(3) Suitable target–motivated perpetrator interaction.

Each system is more than the sum of its parts. This means that when it interacts with another system it adapts.

The value of the suitable target reflects the motivations (needs or goals) of the perpetrator who will respond to the environment

Figure 4.3: The Circles of Analysis: interactions between each complex system

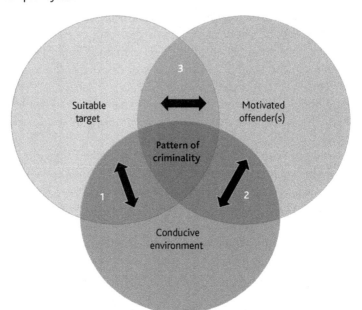

and suitable target in whatever way is necessary to satisfy these needs/meet the goals.

The suitable target's compliance with the perpetrator reflects their own needs (vulnerabilities).

The environment becomes conducive to patterns of abuse and harm when:

- the suitable target is unprotected;
- the perpetrators are unlikely to be caught or sanctioned;
- there is a receptive target.

The exploitation pattern and resultant harm is a stable state. Adaptation is a response to a threat to that stability. An intervention in any of the three systems will trigger adaptation – this will be either adaptive or competitive. Past successful patterns of adaptation are likely to be repeated which makes new emergent patterns predictable *but* interventions must target all three intersections

Figure 4.4: The Circles of Analysis with the possibility spaces

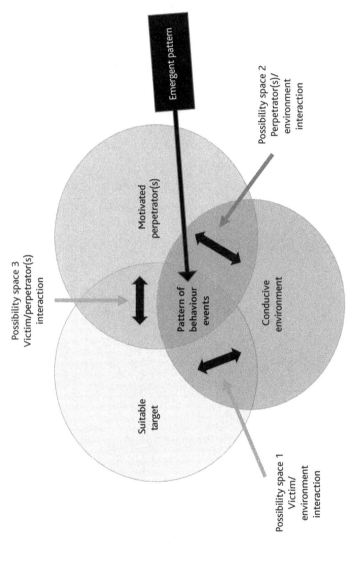

in order to be successful. These areas of intersection, where the dynamics of the relationships occur, are the 'possibility spaces' (see Figure 4.4). I will return to these possibility spaces later but first it is necessary, in the next chapter, to describe and explain what constitutes a 'conducive environment'.

5

Why here? Why now?
The conducive environment

In Chapter 2 I tracked the evolution of terminology and definitions of trafficking and modern slavery, highlighting the challenges this has presented to academics, legislators and policy makers throughout the world. At the end of the chapter, I proposed putting those definitions aside and introduced work that has recently been undertaken by Professor Simon Green, Dr Alicia Heys and myself to develop a definition of 'exploitation' (Green, Heys, and Barlow, forthcoming). We applied this definition of exploitation to explain the importance of the environment in which exploitation is most likely to occur and be maintained over time, developing a concept that we have called the *conducive environment*. This conceptual space describes and explains an ecology in which specific conditions combine that make exploitation of people more (or less) possible by facilitating (or inhibiting) the behaviours, interactions and social systems that lead to the emergence and fluctuation of patterns of exploitation.

Conceptualising exploitation

In developing this concept, we focused on exploitation not only in terms of trafficking and modern slavery but also more generally to capture a range of practices (such as wage suppression, excessive working hours and dangerous working conditions) that exploited certain groups in different contexts. For that reason, we have defined *exploitation* as: 'using a position of power or privilege to unfairly benefit at the expense of a disadvantaged person or group'.

This is not limited to financial benefit or gain and can include gain in terms of power, well-being or any other benefit. Neither is this limited to interpersonal exploitation and can just as easily be applied to institutional and commercial contexts.

The trafficking of people for the purposes of exploitation relies on a fundamental power imbalance between the traffickers and those who are the victims of exploitation. Those who may be suitable targets for exploitation are also likely to be those with the least power or at least fewest resources to protect themselves within their wider social environment. This is especially important to recognise as it enables us to address systemic and structural conditions in the framing of exploitative scenarios, where exploitation is not necessarily only perpetrated by an individual or group of individuals.

Regional case example: Vietnam

By 2020 Vietnam's economic year-on-year growth had increased at a rapid rate, but the distribution of wealth had been uneven and skewed towards urban areas. This increased the economic disparity between cities and rural areas and contributed to rising unemployment in the provinces. This has resulted in increased internal migration to urban areas and migration to other countries. Cross-border migration for work has been positively encouraged by the Vietnamese Government.

Typically, illicit (smuggled) migrants and trafficking victims, themselves of low economic standing, come from small towns and villages in economically depressed, rural areas with high unemployment. Many people living in poorer provinces often lack formal education. Even in rapidly developing areas with high levels of recorded employment, many people are either under-employed or in very insecure employment. The experience of NGOs such as Alliance Anti-Traffic (AAT)[1] and Pacific Links Foundation is that many girls and women who are trafficked left education at

---

[1]   AAT is networked with 24 countries. Illegal trade and direct or online illegal transactions involving children and women are borderless and require strong international connections. The organisation cooperates with ARLEMP (Asian Region Law Enforcement Management Programme) under the Australian Federal Police and, RMIT University, and with the EMPACT

14 seeking work, often to support their families. Additionally, many of these girls and young women had behavioural issues, were unhappy at home and were therefore vulnerable to being trafficked in the first place. For these reasons and others, trafficking networks tend to recruit extensively in rural areas but analysis of National Referral Mechanism (NRM) files by Silverstone and Brickell for the UK Independent Anti-Slavery Commissioner's Office found that the majority of Vietnamese victims of modern slavery identified in the UK had come from the Red River Delta and North Central Coast regions prior to departure from Vietnam (Silverstone and Brickell, 2017).

Common vulnerability factors exploited by traffickers include: unemployment and perceived job opportunities overseas; unhappy domestic situation (for example, the victim may be in an abusive situation, their family may be in debt or there may be an addict in the family); and relatives and friends living in the destination country (CEOP and the British Embassy, Hanoi, 2011).

Traffickers may be connected to friends and family members of those they seek to recruit, and on occasion may actually be connected directly to the victim.

Case example: Linh

Linh grew up in a small city in the Red River Delta region of Vietnam. She was raised by her mother and father and has two younger siblings. She described her childhood as settled and 'normal, like any other family'.

Linh completed her formal education, staying at school until 18 and then entering her vocational training as a tailor in a province of north-eastern Vietnam.

Her training lasted a year. She married her husband at the age of 23. She knew him as a neighbour and he worked as a builder. Her first daughter was born after the first year of marriage and following the birth she stopped working to care for her child.

---

project combating child sexual exploitation under INTERPOL–EUROPOL, and the French Ministry of Interior.

The marriage ran into difficulties after about two years. Linh explained that her husband began drinking heavily and that they were struggling financially. She separated from him in 2013 and returned to live with her parents. She says she sought work at this time but was not able to earn as much as she needed.

Linh was encouraged by a friend to respond to an advertisement from an agency that offered work abroad and promised to arrange transport and accommodation in addition to finding work. The Vietnamese Government has positively encouraged migration for work and there are many state sponsored migration brokers established to assist would-be migrants in pursuit of employment in other countries. However, there are agencies that are corrupt and others that are fronts for organised criminals intending to smuggle or traffic human beings for exploitation. It is not clear whether Linh knew that the agent that she dealt with was criminal or whether she intended to travel illegally (to be smuggled) but confirmed that she paid the equivalent of £31,000 (€35,791 or USD $39,428) in exchange for travel, accommodation and employment. The agent required her passport, birth certificate and identity card.

The money was raised by her parents through loans. Linh was asked if she had considered this an extraordinary amount of money. She explained that the agency had told her and her family that while it was a lot of money, she would earn sufficient to not only pay it back but to make a profit after two years. It was sold to them as an investment.

Linh had enjoyed a stable and settled upbringing and early adulthood. She and her husband lived with her parents-in-law while they were together. She described arguments with her husband over money and his drinking. She also described a difficult relationship with her parents in law who, she said, would often be very critical of her, would make up false stories about her and would frequently shout at her. She admitted that her husband on occasions had slapped her face but said that this did not hurt her but expressed greater distress at the constant criticism of her by her mother- and father-in-law. Because of these problems she made the decision to leave her husband and she agreed to her children remaining in the care of their paternal grandparents. She found this very difficult but maintained weekly contact with them. She left her husband and returned to live with her parents but felt very sad. She tried to find work but had difficulty earning enough money.

Linh was not from an especially vulnerable demographic given that she comes from an apparently stable family background and has had a good education, including vocational training. However, the change in her living conditions following the breakdown of her marriage gave rise to her vulnerability, which must be understood in the context of Vietnamese culture and gender expectations. While Vietnam has quite robust and progressive equalities legislation and social policies, this is not always reflected in cultural values and social norms in which the rule of law is often considered secondary to customs and tradition (Duong, 2001). Traditionally in Vietnam, there is an expectation of women to work diligently to better themselves and their families and to put the needs of their family ahead of their own. Women often feel personally responsible when their family fails to live up to social and cultural norms (Schuler et al, 2006). In both northern and southern Vietnam, families are primarily patriarchal and patrilineal in structure and tradition and married couples often live with the husband's parents during the first few years of their marriage.

There are similarities here with the situation that enabled Zuhaila Alim to be trapped in domestic servitude within the context of her marriage. The conducive environment was the family home, her isolation from the wider community and her own family and the distorted application of gendered traditions and cultural norms enforced by Suhail Alim and his family.

Regional case example: Central and Eastern Europe

Trafficking of children for petty crime and begging is particularly well established in Central and Eastern Europe and most commonly affects the Roma communities in countries such as Romania, Slovakia, the Czech Republic, Hungary and Bulgaria. These communities suffer particularly high levels of poverty and unemployment and have a long history of marginalisation and discrimination.

Historically, there have been high levels of multi-generational street homelessness among Roma people meaning that they often have no identification, rendering them invisible to state records (European Roma Rights Centre and People In Need, 2011; Ravnbøl, 2019). People living in extreme poverty do not have bank accounts and this is true for the Roma who have little option but to seek loans from moneylenders known as *Kamatari*. These lenders impose harsh and repressive terms to recover the debt, including forcing people to commit crimes such as begging and pickpocketing or forcing parents to traffic their own children for the same purpose, or to hand the child over to traffickers (Brotherton and Waters, 2013). Family complicity in trafficking of children for all forms of exploitation has been noted by the European Roma Rights Centre (ERRC) and People in Need (2011), whereby the child was usually recruited for exploitation by a close family member, or friends and associates with close family ties; furthermore, the report found that involvement of the sale of children by parents had also occurred.

In other circumstances families may send their children overseas for a better life and may not be aware that they are being exploited or forced to commit crime. Some children are accompanied by parents or family members who may force them to beg or steal. In some instances, where family members (for example, parents) make a child beg or to steal the child may understand this to be 'for the good of the family' making them feel valued or useful (Ballet et al, 2002).

A number of factors may drive people into the hands of traffickers. Domestic violence and substance abuse are common. Gender-based violence, as a form of sex discrimination and violence against children, has been found to be a significant contributing factor to women being trafficked. Elsewhere domestic violence and chaotic households have also been associated with child abuse and neglect which can push children towards sexual and criminal exploitation (Knowsley Council, 2015; European Roma Rights Centre and People In Need, 2011). Substance abuse has been found in all age groups within the Roma community even as young as 6 years old, especially among homeless street children. Drugs have also been identified as being used by traffickers to recruit addicted parents so that some young people or children are passed or sold to traffickers in order to maintain a habit or service a debt (European Roma Rights Centre and People In Need, 2011).

In Bulgaria, the Czech Republic, Hungary, Romania and Slovakia, Roma have for generations faced great obstacles to accessing employment due to low levels of education and high levels of discrimination. The lack of employment opportunities and the resulting poverty and social exclusion have been listed in all five countries as the most prevalent vulnerability factors. Lack of education is consistently cited as a problem for Roma and Traveller children both in the UK and in Europe with high dropout rates and disproportionate placement in provisions for children with special educational needs (Bingham, 2010; European Roma Rights Centre and People In Need, 2011).

An uncertain connection between coercion and exploitation

Another important aspect of our definition of exploitation is that it separates coercion and oppression from exploitation. Coercion and oppression are means of exercising domination or control over someone but do not in themselves realise benefit, thus they may lead to exploitation, but exploitation is not reliant upon them. Unlike exploitation, coercion and oppression are always intentional as they are reliant on deception, manipulation, threats and violence. In exploitative circumstances where coercion and oppression are present it is easier to identify exploitation as it is severe, and consequently easier to formulate preventive interventions and remedies.

If exploitation is not reliant on coercion and can be mutually beneficial, how it can be identified and recognised? The answer may be found in looking into the disadvantage that led to the exploitation. In most societies there are forms of institutionalised disadvantage which are part of norms and values. Consequently, some types of disadvantages may sit outside of norms and values of a particular society and can be characterised as 'misfortune or injustice' while other types of disadvantage may be embedded within a culture, further complicating the identification of exploitation.

The definition of exploitation offered in Chapter 2 contains three components: (1) power and privilege, (2) unfair benefit and (3) disadvantage. Power, privilege and disadvantage are governed by structural conditions that shape who is in a position to exploit or be exploited while unfair benefit results from the process of exploitation. These all exist in a constantly adapting ecosystem in which specific circumstances give rise to different opportunities to exploit (or not) and to be exploited (or not).

However, exploitation is also a social practice that can be studied independently of any legal criteria, avoiding the danger of either ethnocentrism, cultural relativism or ideological doctrine (Green, Heys, and Barlow, forthcoming). It carries two important theoretical antecedents which clarify why it occurs. The first has already been discussed: exploitative behaviour is the common denominator across wide and varied forms of human suffering which avoids the presumption of the 'movement', 'coercion' or 'oppression' of people. The second is that precisely because exploitation is widely used and applied within labour relations, it has currency as a justificatory rationale for 'unfair benefit' that is central to our definition. Although that work addressed a general concept of exploitation, I intend to apply this concept to trafficking of human beings and all forms of modern slavery because these practices have, at their core, the exploitation of individuals and groups of people. In other words, trafficking, slavery and slavery-like practices are processes for different patterns of exploitation that are context-specific.

The theory knitting in the development of the conducive environment

Current thinking about trafficking and modern slavery lacks compelling explanatory theory that connects the macro to the micro or explains the social phenomenon of human trafficking, slavery and exploitation in specific contexts. Most theories are located in disparate global economic and political contexts (Bales, 2012), competitive market forces (O'Connell Davidson, 2015) or, to use a term from migration studies, 'push and pull factors' (Cheng, 2017). These foreground the distribution and accumulation of wealth and security but fall short of explanatory power when considering why some people in some contexts are more likely than others to be exploited.

In lieu of this, a list of indicators has emerged that point to issues such as human trafficking such as the ILO Operational Indicators of Trafficking (International Labour Organization, 2009) and the UNODC Human Trafficking Indicators (United Nations Office on Drugs and Crime). These can be useful reference points but describe rather than explain the existence of such practices. So, while we have many estimates of the extent of the problem and a reasonable sense of what it looks like, there is limited understanding of why it happens to particular people in particular places. The *conducive environment* (Barlow, 2019; Barlow et al, 2021; Green, Heys, and Barlow, forthcoming) is a mid-level model that is applied in this chapter to understand why human trafficking and modern slavery tends to be concentrated on certain populations in some places and not others. The model required the knitting together of several diverse theories.

Previous approaches to understanding the problem of trafficking and modern slavery have been hindered by a 'segregative' approach to not only theory development (Kalmar and Sternberg, 1988) but also practice guidance and service design. To overcome this problem, this chapter develops an integrative model of trafficking and modern slavery and, indeed, other forms of exploitation. An integrative theory is one that integrates the best aspects of a set of given theories with one's own ideas regarding the domain under investigation, instead of emphasising those features that discriminate among theories to provide a unifying explanation of the problem (Kalmar and Sternberg, 1988; Ward and Siegert, 2002).

Social embeddedness

This is a concept that is generally associated with social economics. Its core assumption is that people's individual interests as well as their economic activities are embedded within networks of social interactions. Economic outcomes emerge from these interactions. Maurer (2012) advances the theory by arguing for greater consideration of how groups of individual's mutual expectations, which are defined within social relations, are affected by social norms, values and the formal and informal social institutions, are met. Any social activity, economic or otherwise, consists of a sequence of decision-making in pursuit of both individual and group interests.

Effective decision-making depends upon the quality of the information and availability or accessibility of the information to the decision-maker. A social economic system is consequently shaped by the prevailing interests of the most dominant groups within the social institutions who have the greatest control over the flow of information and greater influence over group and individual identity. Maurer (2012, p 493) argues that: 'What really matters is the application of empirical theses about the dominant interest in a specific situation and the problems individuals are facing when trying to pursue their interests.' This leads to a more complex, holistic and realistic understanding of social economic systems at the micro and macro levels. Maurer (2012, p 475) recommends the analysis of 'the interplay of different social mechanisms – social capital, trust, legitimacy, hierarchy, social entrepreneurs – that work either through information in a network, group norms or generalized expectations in a wider institutional framework'.

Focusing on human trafficking and modern slavery, Heys (2023) offers a detailed analysis of how historic and current social structures in different contexts create vulnerabilities by constraining choices and therefore decision-making, and action, for some individuals and groups while creating opportunities for exploitation by dominant individuals and groups.

I accept Maurer's recommendations and approach the concept of social embeddedness in relation to trafficking and modern slavery by combining historical and current empirical work with theoretical arguments. Kelly (2007, p 89) explains in her analysis of human trafficking in Central Asia how 'interconnecting social, political and economic conditions form the fertile fields within which exploitative operators can profit from the misfortunes of others ... Central Asia poignantly extends these connections to the relevance of histories of forced labour/migration and ethnic hierarchies'.

In her assessment of convicted traffickers Rosemary Broad has identified how traffickers and those trafficked for exploitation often shared similar starting points. People become vulnerable to trafficking and exploitation because of social restrictions based upon their backgrounds and experiences. The paucity of available options means that those who are ultimately subjected to abuse and exploitation turn to illegitimate means to meet their basic needs in restricted circumstances (for example, Roma people in Europe turning either to the *Kamatari* moneylenders or to begging and street crime; D in Operation RASTRELLI and some of the women in Operation PELTIER who made decisions to enter sex work, despite the risks involved). Broad's findings suggest that one pathway to becoming a perpetrator starts in similar circumstances to that of becoming a victim; that is, there is a bifurcation point where someone may become a trafficker and exploiter or become trafficked and exploited. The transition from victim to perpetrator occurs as a response to the predicament, being the adoption of predatory solutions (Broad, 2018). In some circumstances it is possible for an individual, such as Hanna in Operation PELTIER who contributed to the monitoring and control of Katarina in Zsolt's house, to occupy the victim and perpetrator space simultaneously (Barlow, 2022).

The conducivity of environmental conditions to the emergence of patterns of exploitation

Old and established patterns of trafficking, modern slavery and other forms of exploitation are concentrated on certain populations of different places over time. Defining exploitation as *this or that being done here and there* does not help us understand or adequately respond to the problem. It must be understood in terms of the contextual mechanisms that enable different patterns of exploitation to emerge, adapt and endure over time (Pawson and Tilley, 1997). The best context to study these patterns as an output of social systems and structures is the local community where the cross-sectional interactions, tensions and power-plays at the core of the problem can be observed (Fuller and Myers, 1941; Barlow et al, 2021).

The degree to which a pattern of exploitation is problematised is determined by the community in which it occurs: domestic servitude and forced labour may receive very little attention in community X, whereas in the neighbouring community Y it is a level of concern approaching moral panic. Child labour, for instance, has been problematised by the UN based upon largely Western assumptions about childhood and concepts of exploitation (Ballet et al, 2002). However, as discussed in Chapters 2 and 3, constructs such as childhood are culturally determined and vary throughout history. A geographical and economic environment may necessitate children engaging in labour in order for the family to survive (Barlow, 2019) but, as Ballet argues, a child who works to support the family also may gain status within their family and community, providing services and gaining skills that develop the child's social capital into adulthood.

In his work on Italian Mafia structures in America in the 1960s, Cressey (1969) observes that at a community street level, organised crime rackets were tolerated if the community perceived some benefit and little risk to its welfare and cohesion. This tolerance grew through all levels of society so that the Mafia corrupted law enforcement and politics, threatening the integrity of social institutions and the stability of society as a whole. Only when the Mafia and organised crime became an existential threat to society was there a constituency of support to reorganise against organised crime and, in turn, forcing the Italian Mafia in the US to reorganise, redefine its purpose and seek new alliances. Mafias and organised crime structures and their outputs are a product of their historical embeddedness within the socio-geographical environments in which they began (Sergi, 2017). The same is true of all social systems and subsystems. Sociological and criminological research that has sought to investigate trafficking and exploitation of human beings has largely failed to do more than develop definitions and typologies of exploitation, such as that provided by Cooper, Hesketh, Ellis, and Fair (2017).

Research into different forms of exploitation as a social problem has tended to treat exploitation as a series of objective items (such as incidence, kinds of people involved in the problem, their number, types and social characteristics), a reductive Newtonian epistemology that reduces the problem into such supposedly objective elements in the belief that this captures the central character of exploitation and constitutes scientific analysis (Barlow, 2019). Furthermore, this is an erroneous assumption that undermines most policy and justice responses to the problem. Blumer argued that 'a social problem exists only in terms of how it is defined and conceived in a society instead of being an objective condition with a definitive make-up' (Blumer, 1971).

Human trafficking and modern slavery emerges as an output of complex social systems – its patterns result from the interactions between a vast number of components which organise according to a simple set of rules. These rules are informed by latent, dormant or potential events in the local area. Before it can rise to local consciousness, debate and control, a local issue or event is essential to trigger the necessary contextual mechanisms going, to activate systemic processes that result in patterns of exploitation. The tensions, social values and transactions that make up the problem of exploitation once it has emerged are, according to Fuller and Myers, similar in all communities but can only be fully evaluated and understood as it functions in the local situation (Fuller and Myers, 1941).

The arguments of Fuller and Myers, as well as Cressey, Blumer and Manson, support a conclusion that exploitation of individuals and groups by other individuals and groups emerges as a social problem from the cultural organisation of the community and the applications of its approved values. The patterns of exploitation that concern us here are in fact normal human behaviours rather than deviance from what is perceived as normal or proper in a civilised society but are shaped and determined by the environments in which they occur. The environmental mechanisms that trigger systemic processes to produce patterns of exploitation are disruption, isolation, entitlement and desperation (Green, Heys, and Barlow, forthcoming).

The pattern of exploitation that emerges is determined by the proximity of the suitable targets for exploitation and those that are motivated to perpetrate the exploitation, but also parts and subsystems within the environment that are not a direct part of the process of exploitation but contribute to the conditions in which it can be maintained.

The emergence of trafficking and modern slavery in different places and at different times may be confounding because there are many control parameters with potential interactions and intervention can result in unintended or unfamiliar feedback loops creating unexpected effects for both good and ill. Each new measure to counter trafficking and modern slavery is likely to be unreliable (that is, what works in one context at a given time may not be effective in another). This is one reason why lists of trafficking and slavery indicators and prevalence statistics, typologies and 'risk factors' are of limited use unless we understand how constellations of these factors result from different types of interactions under a range of conditions.

6

Possibility spaces: tightening and loosening of environments and interactions

Exploitation is a pattern of transactions that emerges from the synergistic, dynamic relationships between the exploiters and the exploited. These interactions are autonomous as every person, as a component of a social system, has their own motivations and needs which will drive them towards perceived opportunities to meet those needs. Other individuals or groups that have synergistic needs and motivations will endeavour to attract them to join. Exploitation may therefore refer to patterns of complex behaviour that emerge from local interactions between system components over time (Manson, 2001). These interactions for the most part follow linear pathways or sequences as part of a process. Such pathways may be simple (in that they have a very small number of stages in them for attainment of a goal or completion of a process) or complicated (with many stages or steps towards attainment of a goal or completion of a process).

Linear interactions can be characterised as those that are expected in a familiar process or sequence and even unplanned interactions and events along that pathway are visible and comprehensible (Perrow, 1999). For example, a regular journey to the workplace may encounter an unexpected event when a burst water main has flooded a road, requiring a diversion along a different route. Both the journey (the process of getting to work) and the cause of the interruption to the journey is a familiar one – it is visible and comprehensible and the effect of the burst water main has a clear series of effects which can be mitigated and finally resolved. Once resolved, things will usually get back to normal pretty quickly.

Complex interactions are those that occur in unfamiliar sequences and are either not visible or not immediately comprehensible (Perrow, 1999). For example, the journey to work has been delayed as traffic slows, then stops, backing up for miles then suddenly and inexplicably starts moving again.

Proximity and indirect information, as sociologist Charles Perrow explains, are two other sources of complex interactions.

> The much more common interactions, the kind we intuitively try to construct because of their simplicity and comprehensibility, I will call linear interactions. Linear interactions overwhelmingly predominate in all systems. But even the most linear of systems will have at least one source of complex interactions, the environment, since it impinges upon many parts or units of the system. (Perrow, 1999, p 75)

Exploitation through trafficking and modern slavery is a sequence of complex interactions of systems and sub-systems that have numerous branching pathways, feedback loops and the ability to jump from one linear sequence to another. The connections between system components are not only adjacent but also a serial sequence of interactions that can multiply, creating a network as other components are reached and become connected. Systems that grow in terms of their size and the functions they serve, within ever more challenging environments, respond to new opportunities for growth and threats to stability. They experience ever more incomprehensible or unexpected interactions – interactions that are hard to comprehend because they are not visible or measurable.

While knowledge and experience has helped us begin to describe human trafficking and modern slavery, it is not very well understood. This is probably because it is not an objective, single and measurable event or product but a transformational process that responds to new or changing conditions over time and place. Many of its processes and interactions between victims, perpetrators and their environments are hidden and therefore largely incomprehensible.

Tight and loose interactions

'Tight coupling' is a term used in engineering and mechanics that refers to there being no slack or 'give' between two items so that what happens to or within one directly affects what happens in the other. Perrow (1999) and other organisational theorists have elaborated this term to describe and explain the responsiveness of systems to shocks or destabilisation or the failure of component parts. Loosely coupled systems can incorporate shocks and failures or pressures to change with little or no destabilisation because the loose connections can make it easier to isolate a component that isn't working properly and either simplify remedial action or increase the range of available interventions without impacting the rest of the system. This also allows a loosely coupled system to grow or be made more efficient and evolve more readily. The downside of this is that loosely coupled systems become more complex. Inevitably communication between components becomes increasingly difficult and indirect so that coordination is less controlled: because loosely coupled system components (for our purposes, that is to say people) have fewer mutual dependencies, they need to communicate more to exchange information, which can slow down the operation of the system, increase the risk of miscommunication and infiltration from outside sources of interference.

By contrast a tightly coupled system has a set of clear rules to which all components (the people that make up that organisational system) adhere and the rules are enforced by an inspection and feedback system. Tightly coupled systems can respond more quickly to new pressures and shocks because they are quickly and easily coordinated and follow a playbook that is established, well rehearsed and understood by everyone within the organisational system. However, such systems are brittle and lack flexibility when the nature or causes of the shock are unexpected or not understood (incomprehensible). A crisis occurs when all previous existing strategies no longer work. Tightly coupled systems continue to enact their established and familiar rules and processes which will work only for as long as the emergency is within the knowledge and experience of the organisation, otherwise the response of the system can have disastrous consequences.

Gelfland et al (2011) have used similar concepts to describe a divide between 'tight and loose cultures', where the former have low tolerances of deviant behaviour and strong social norms, and the latter have high tolerances of deviant behaviour and weak social norms. Drawing on these concepts, Green, Heys and I (forthcoming) have further elaborated these ideas in terms of social bonds to describe *conducive environments* as those spaces where social bonds are either too tight or loose to an extent that allows for exploitation to occur. Gelfland et al (2011, p 1100) describe cultures (societal or organisational) where:

> Tightness-looseness is part of a complex, loosely integrated multilevel system that comprises distal ecological and historical threats (for example, high population density, resource scarcity, a history of territorial conflict, and disease and environmental threats), broad versus narrow socialization in societal institutions (for example, autocracy, media regulations), the strength of everyday recurring situations, and micro-level psychological affordances (for example, prevention self-guides, high regulatory strength, need for structure).

Drawing on Gelfland et al's (2011) concept we propose that there is a set of common mechanisms which can precipitate exploitation as a result of events such as war, food and energy shortage, economic or political crisis, pathogenic threat and natural disaster within environments. These are all environmental shocks that can trigger mechanisms that increase the tightening or loosening of social bonds and, in turn, lead to the emergence of patterns of exploitation. These mechanisms are:

- disruption;
- isolation;
- entitlement; and
- desperation.

Disruption

We use *disruption* to refer to what might be an instantaneous, deliberate or accidental event that invigorates or demoralises a community or society that had been used to operating under stable, predictable, normal conditions (Blum, 1996). Disruption to an environment and its systems is not in and of itself wholly negative, being a necessary trigger for adaptation or change with the potential for greater resilience (Warren et al, 1998; Woodward, 2019). Systems that remain in a permanent state of equilibrium deplete life-sustaining resources in their environment and ultimately decline and burn out (Warren, Franklin, and Streeter, 1998). Disruption that generates change can generate opportunities for positive growth which also tends to increase the complexity of social systems (Pycroft and Bartollas, 2014), such as businesses and markets, the institutions of government, the military, law and justice, health and medicine, education and social welfare (Blum, 1996). While such disruption can create opportunities for beneficial change, there are always unintended consequences which include negative impacts on minorities and new opportunities for crime and exploitation (Cooray, 2017).

Different patterns of disruption occur at different levels of the physical and social environment; for example, at the individual or family level, community and societal level, and the global level. The effects of disruption and the way social systems react and adapt do not follow a neat, linear, causal pathway. Social systems are complex, meaning that they have vast numbers of actors whose interactions with each other, and their environments are permanently in flux, adapting and changing to a variety of internal and external stimuli (Manson, 2001). Consequently, the effects of disruption, the perturbation created throughout complex social systems causes the effects to travel in multiple directions simultaneously, to be 'non-linear' and complex (Warren et al, 1998; Manson, 2001; Pycroft and Bartollas, 2014), resulting in varied opportunities and patterns of exploitation (Fatić, 1999; Kelly, 2007; Broad, 2018).

Disruption leading to exploitation through the loosening of social bonds

Disruption could refer to any event that significantly impacts upon usual daily living, ranging from a family breakdown (as in the case of Linh) to a major disaster such as the Haitian earthquake of 2010. Crucially, it interrupts a person's trajectory in a way that increases their vulnerability (Hassett and Stevens, 2014).

The decline or complete failure of systems of regulation and control weakens social ties as resource allocation is de-centralised, social support through kin and community institutions is dispersed, forcing people to seek new sources of support, guidance and information (Cooray, 2017; Samarasinghe, 2003). This generates new networks and relational power imbalances by which those with the greater power have unfair advantage over those with less power to achieve their own ends.

When Russia escalated its invasion of Ukraine to a full-scale war in February 2022 it forced the external displacement of over 5.8 million Ukrainian people and an additional 7.1 million internally by the end of April that year. Women and children accounted for more than 90 per cent of those displaced, with the majority of men conscripted and required to stay behind (US Department of State, 2022). The war triggered disruptive perturbations globally affecting international and irregular migration flows, inflationary pressures, food and energy shortages and the reorganisation of supply chains.

War is a disruption event which leads to impairment or complete failure of systems of control, resulting in displacement, reordering of political priorities, structural change, increased living costs, unemployment and privatisation of services. Individuals may experience just one of these effects of disruption or, more likely, may suffer from a combination simultaneously or over time. War can cause a catastrophic breakdown of systems of control, whereby paternalistic systems of support are abandoned as priorities rapidly change, leaving individuals without guidance, information, social support or access to welfare.

Disruption leading to exploitation through the tightening of social bonds

Social systems enter a state of crisis when disruption threatens to overwhelm the usual mechanisms for maintaining the stability and integrity of social order, institutions and governance. Society may seek leadership that offers clarity and structure rapidly or become frustrated and angry with those in authority for causing, or failing to provide protection from, the disruption. This can lead to tightening of laws, regulations and sanctions by the authorities presented as decisive action and often supported by a social majority seeking strong leadership and reassurance. In this climate, in the face of a real or imagined threat to social cohesion, populism and authoritarianism gains traction.

As Neuborne (2019) observes of authoritarian populists and dictators 'there's always a charismatic leader, a disaffected mass, an adroit use of communications media, economic insecurity, racial or religious fault lines, xenophobia, a turn to violence, and a search for scapegoats' (Neuborne, 2019, p 33). The effect marginalises individuals and groups, neutralising their identities as potential victims of abuse, exploitation and violence. While this is not an issue tied to any single geographical location, and is applicable the world over, an example of this can be found in the portrayal of refugees and asylum seekers as illegal migrants or security threats, characterising welfare claimants as the feckless antithesis of hard-working families (Tihelková, 2015) and support agencies, human rights lawyers and judges who support them are defamed enemies of the people (McMillan, 2022).

Disruption simultaneously creates opportunities for those who offer to facilitate escape or protection to obtain positions by which they are able to control information and resources and consolidate their power. The effects are felt most severely in the least resilient countries (Frontex, 2021) creating opportunities for those who are sufficiently motivated to exploit people, resources and circumstances for their own ends, be they benign or mendacious. As an example, the Haitian 'restavec' system of child servitude is deeply rooted in Haitian Creole culture and history. 'Restavec' is a Haitian Creole word meaning 'stay with'. Children that are taken into domestic servitude tend to be from extremely poor, often rural, families. They may be said to be 'staying with relatives', 'temporarily helping another family', 'away at school' or 'boarding with a wealthier friend' (Janak, 2000). The Haitian earthquake of 2010 and subsequent cholera outbreak orphaned many children and separated more from families and carers, making them easy targets for child traffickers and local practices such as restavec 'allowed' families to take in children and use them for domestic labour (Gurung and Clarke, 2018). There was a sparsely regulated open Haitian/ Dominican border with the two national governments only monitoring a few major crossing points. Subsequently, many individuals regularly cross the border illegally which, according to the Working Group on the UPR [Universal Periodic Review] Human Rights Council, enabled the easy removal of Haitian children to the Dominican Republic and abroad (Freedom and des Avocats Internationaux, 2011).

Isolation

In traditional, pre-modern societies, people's lives were closely tied to their place within a clan or class, and they had limited capacity to deviate from the circumstances into which they were born. The Industrial Revolution ushered in increasing specialisation of labour, which brought with it changes to traditional forms of social life that separated labour from community and created the conditions for social mobility and meritocracy (Barlow, 2019; Green, Heys, and Barlow, forthcoming). Despite these societal changes, our life decisions aren't made in a vacuum and we remain interdependent on other human beings to provide meaning, belonging and support. We rely on friends, family, colleagues and acquaintances to discuss our plans with and whom we rely on for opinions, advice and information.

Isolation leading to exploitation through the loosening of social bonds

In situations of weakened support networks, individuals become isolated from the people they would depend upon in times of need. Individuals must make decisions to act based upon their own knowledge and previous experience. This is a loosening of social bonds. It may enable an individual to seek information from a wider range of sources and freedom to seek opportunities elsewhere (Lui et al, 2017), but an individual has only their own experience, personal resources and subjective knowledge to make their decisions. A loosening of social bonds within the social environment increases the possibility of the isolation of some, while also increasing the opportunity for their exploitation by others; these loose bonds, lack of regulation and feedback loops then allow these possibilities to thrive unchecked.

In environments with loose social bonds, social cohesion is more fragile, there is a lack of collectivism and fewer shared goals, and individualism can increase the likelihood of isolation and marginalisation of individual people and minority groups. Such environments can generate opportunities for exploitation at the level of the individual or community, by groups, organisations, social institutions or states.

In these situations, perpetrators of exploitation more easily identify those in need of support. For example, economic migrants and refugees may have become isolated from their support networks and are travelling alone, without clear knowledge of where they are going or how to get there. They become suitable targets for those looking to exploit others: predatory exploiters can begin to access and gain the trust of these individuals by offering assistance, perhaps support in crossing a border, accommodation or employment.

For example, there is growing evidence of organised crime groups (OCGs) impersonating NGOs in Ukraine in an attempt to coax vulnerable individuals towards them with offers of assistance (Rosenzweig-Ziff et al, 2022). In 2022, in the immediate aftermath of the full-scale invasion of Ukraine by the Russian Federation, Europol noted that the highest risk of trafficking from Ukraine was at the borders, with traffickers approaching those who were being displaced with offers of immediate support (Europol, 2022). It is important to re-emphasise that this is but one example of an issue that has no geographical boundaries. With the World Bank's estimation that over 143 million people will have been displaced due to climate change in sub-Saharan Africa, South Asia and Latin America by 2050 (Clement et al, 2021), traffickers will have the opportunity to operationalise this approach of luring the displaced into exploitation with false offers of support the world over. In such situations, where the vulnerable have no support networks and no safe options, they are often left in circumstances where they have little choice but to accept offers of support from strangers, even if they are cognisant that the offers may not be entirely legitimate (Heys, 2023).

Isolation leading to exploitation through the tightening of social bonds

While the conditions described in the previous section depict how isolation can increase the risk of exploitation by loosening social bonds, on the opposite side of the fulcrum, the tightening of social bonds can also increase isolation and the risk of exploitation. Tightening of social bonds can facilitate group cohesion; identity and shared goals; collective action to achieve those goals (Gelfland et al, 2011); and tightening of rules, social structures and norms for the collective good. This tightening also restricts general knowledge within a social environment and inhibits independent thought, creativity, identification of alternative goals or innovative new routes to achieving those goals. If the holders of power tighten their control of information and its flow to, and within, the social network then they can suppress dissent, decide the goals and isolate those that do not service their objectives. Tighter bonds reduce the possibility for individuals to seek their information from more diverse sources and engage with people outside of their immediate social network. They also limit migration and social change. As we have seen in the previous chapters and case studies, once suitable targets for exploitation have been identified and ensnared, the traffickers concentrate on tightening bonds with the victim to first of all increase their isolation, build dependence upon the trafficker and ultimately achieve total dominance over the victim.

To achieve this, perpetrators identify the unmet health, physical, safety and social needs of their targets, and ensnare them by appearing able to meet these needs (Wood, 2019). Victims may come to trust their abuser and become increasingly dependent upon them. The victim is systematically further isolated from other people or support networks that might otherwise protect them (such as friends and family), and the coercive control increases to the point at which the perpetrators achieve complete dominance of the victim including their movements, where they live, when and if they eat and sleep, even their beliefs about their situation (Barlow, 2017; Zahir et al, 2020). It is common within the context of such exploitative relationships both at an individual and community or social level, because of their controlling characteristics, for victims to be simultaneously terrified of, and entirely dependent upon, the person exploiting them (Cantor and Price, 2007; van der Watt and van der Westhuizen, 2017).

In 2020, governments around the world imposed various degrees of isolation measures as part of their national strategies to prevent the spread of COVID-19 infection, emphasising the necessity of compliance for the collective good. This ranged from the closure of borders to local restrictions on movement and social contact. These measures had negative economic impacts, impeding supply chains and opportunities for people to seek employment. This affected some communities more severely than others; for example, the densely populated *favela* communities in Latin America that suffer from inadequate social policy, inconsistent investment and underfunding of health care, education, utilities and little trust in law enforcement and its ability to protect citizens (Davis and Hilgers, 2022). Under these conditions, well-established OCGs, factions and cartels established themselves in quasi-governance roles through a combination of violent intimidation and corruption while engaging in extortion of businesses, kidnap and drug trafficking. For such groups, the pandemic provided opportunities to augment their existing power and control (Berg and Varsori, 2020; Aziani et al, 2023).

In Brazil, President Jair Bolsonaro was reluctant to close borders and downplayed the seriousness of the pandemic despite the rising death toll, especially high in impoverished *favelas*. This provided the OCGs an opportunity to expand their governance by tightening social bonds within the *favelas* by stepping in to impose local lockdowns and curfews. Because the criminal groups had members operating and living in these areas, they were attuned to the needs, problems and goals of the community, families and individuals. The OCGs provided makeshift health care services, attended to infrastructure problems, such as maintaining utility supplies and community buildings, while enforcing people's compliance with their rules, and exploiting illicit markets such as the sex industry, drugs markets and other criminal enterprises with little resistance from citizens or officials (Baker and Leão, 2021; Davis and Hilgers, 2022).

Aziani et al (2023) draw attention to the way in which criminal organisations tighten social bonds in this way, explaining:

It is plausible that the provision of goods in high demand is primarily intended to strengthen bonds with the local population while discrediting legitimate institutions, highlighting the inability on national and local government to help the community ... OCGs seek to maximize their audiences, thus obtaining higher returns on their investments. Likewise, by enforcing lockdowns and stay-at-home orders, OCGs try to propose themselves as socially legitimated governing institutions. All these actions are functional to obtaining a bottom-up legitimization. (p 128)

Entitlement

As Green, Heys and I outlined in our definition of exploitation, a power imbalance between victim and perpetrator is a prerequisite for all situations of exploitation. However, for this power imbalance to be exploited, it needs to exist in an environment which allows for it to occur with impunity: the exercise of privilege without consequence. While this may occur in situations where people can act with impunity because there is too little regulation of privilege (loosening), it may equally occur where there is too much protection of privilege (tightening). The under- or over-regulated social hierarchy creates the conditions for exploitation through the unconstrained exercise of privilege which combines with the suppression of aspirations of the underprivileged.

Entitlement and the loosening of social bonds

Entitlement, which leads to exploitation through the loosening of social bonds, is best understood as a situation in which individuals identify an opportunistic prerogative to operate with impunity. This allows them to benefit from a power imbalance, which places them in a preferable situation to others and where there is little likelihood that there will be repercussions for perpetrating exploitation. Significant under-regulating of a system contributes to an environment that is more conducive to the emergence of patterns of exploitation.

If a system is particularly permissive, it can lead to those in a position of power fostering a sense of individualism where they promote their own self-interest above the interests of others, where these actions are accepted by society. Because of the position such individuals hold, any attempts to regulate that behaviour are simply ignored, or rules re-written.

A growing body of literature details how peacekeeping troops contribute to, are sometimes directly involved in and are very rarely held accountable for exploiting others – particularly women and girls in the form of sexual exploitation. Some of this research has identified how criminal networks begin to traffic women and girls into regions once it is known that peacekeeping troops will be introduced. Despite peacekeepers being forbidden from paying for sex, the troops bring with them a great demand and money presenting criminal networks with an illicit market opportunity (Picarelli, 2002; Amnesty International, 2004; Kelly, 2022). These studies also discovered that local increases in human trafficking are directly proportionate to the size of the foreign force, making a compelling link between peacekeeping missions and human trafficking (Picarelli, 2002; Amnesty International, 2004; Smith and Miller-de la Cuesta, 2011).

While there is regulation in these environments, in terms of what peacekeepers are and are not permitted to do, the peacekeepers are there to maintain the law and, as such, they are in charge. Despite plentiful evidence of troops having been found to have paid for sex, or using their power to financially benefit directly from transporting victims, facilitating their travel across borders and stamping their documents (Picarelli, 2002), they are very rarely held accountable for their actions (Vandenberg, 2018; Pehlic, 2020). When they are reprimanded, punishment is rarely more serious than repatriation (Amnesty International, 2004; Pehlic, 2020). They have an opportunistic prerogative to act with impunity.

Entitlement and the tightening of social bonds

While loosening of social bonds can create situations in which those in power find the opportunistic prerogative to act with impunity, the tightening of social bonds may also create situations in which individuals are able to exercise power without consequence; however, this is a hierarchical, rather than an opportunistic, privilege.

In the UK, those seeking asylum are predominantly prohibited from undertaking paid employment while they wait for the outcome of their asylum application. In the meantime, they are provided with a small stipend (currently £45 per week) on which to live. A prominent two-year research project identified that forms of extremely exploitative labour were often unavoidable for those in the asylum system for them to be able to meet their basic human needs (Lewis et al, 2014; Dwyer et al, 2016). The lack of right to work, coupled with inadequate support, means that such individuals often have little choice but to turn to unscrupulous individuals willing to employ them illegally and who may see the employment of asylum seekers (and other unregularised migrants) as a way to make profit. In such a scenario the power imbalance between exploiter and exploited is exacerbated because the hierarchy generated by the asylum system leaves the asylum seeker with no power to negotiate wages, hours or working conditions. Unscrupulous employers with an unchallenged level of power and a degree of entitlement in which they can confidently recruit and exploit others' labour to their maximum benefit know that the people they are hiring are unlikely to report poor conditions because of the repercussions of doing so, thus exploiting their workers using their vulnerable immigration status as a means of control. In such a situation the asylum seeker is entirely at the mercy of the employers and has no recourse to support should the situation become exploitative or dangerous. Policy is such that should an asylum seeker be found to have been working when the system prohibits them from doing so, they will be arrested and detained for breaking the conditions of the asylum system.

Desperation

Human motivation is, according to Maslow ([1943] 2014), driven by biological, psychological, emotional and social needs. These needs are the stimuli that drive or inhibit behaviour with the aim of gratifying or satiating the need.

According to rational choice theory (Clarke and Cornish, 1985), human beings are essentially rational actors that make choices based upon a rapid cost/benefit analysis, which is based upon the available information and beliefs of the decision-maker (Elster, 2001), but this assertion must be made with certain caveats. As Hodgson explains, it is necessary to distinguish between claims that people 'maximise manifest payoffs' and claims that people 'maximise utility' (2012, p 94). Whether or not a decision is considered risky or harmful (and to whom) is greatly influenced by previous experiences, values and knowledge of the decision-maker; the conditions under which their decision must be made; and their capacity to frame, identify and analyse options (Sykes and Matza, 2013; Byrne and Callaghan, 2014; Jennings, 2014). This type of constrained choice, cost–benefit analysis and assessment of utility is epitomised by D's decision-making in the case study Operation RASTRELLI.

Under adverse conditions, human decision-making and behaviour tends to lead to immediate and extreme loss aversion: gains and losses are interpreted by the decision-maker based upon their goals or desired outcomes (Jennings, 2014). If the pressure to act is sufficient, the decision-maker may take the 'least-worst option' or decide that to meet their immediate needs, a risk is worth taking. If the motivating needs for the decision-maker relate to survival (food, shelter, safety) then the urgency of these needs will prioritise them over the higher-level needs of affiliation and esteem. We saw in Operation FORT and Operation PELTIER how the traffickers, at the recruitment stage, pressurised their targets to make a quick decision on whether to travel with them, pressing them with a time-limited offer, the need to travel that day and so forth.

The desperate survival decisions of people living in marginalised groups, in extreme poverty, the displaced and dispossessed, increase their visibility and vulnerability to those who will commodify them for a worldwide market that wants cheap goods and services (Samarasinghe, 2003). And so, we come to the fourth and final predisposing characteristic of the conducive environment: desperation. Desperation is an important component in decision-making, especially in high-stress situations, where the resultant actions are attempts to establish or regain control over what appears to be an uncontrollable situation (Hannan and Hackathorn, 2022).

Desperation leading to exploitation through the loosening of social bonds

Loose environments are more likely to adhere to neoliberal ideology that emphasises economic freedom with a view to greater economic and social progress for individuals. Policies encourage free enterprise, de-regulation, individual responsibility, globalisation, reduction in trade union power and greater flexibility in employment (Gelfland et al, 2011). However, such policies have been criticised as increasing inequalities and widening the socio-economic gap between the richest and poorest (Samarasinghe, 2003; Morgan, 2010; Cooray, 2017). In unequal societies, insecurity of housing, personal finances, social security, health care and the future of the welfare state is wider-spread and the perceived need to self-protect is greater, exacerbating fear and anxiety.

The loosening effect of globalisation has led to greater movement of people and commodities and opportunities for emerging economies to access developed countries and markets, and has arguably improved living standards, gender equality, human rights and enabled labour migration to affluent countries, although in-country economic inequalities have increased (Potrafke, 2015). Despite such benefits, specific populations continue to live in extreme poverty and are increasingly marginalised. Increased economic inequality ensures a supply of desperately poor people who are bought and sold to serve the demands of cheap labour, exploitative sex or forced criminality.

Desperation leading to exploitation through the tightening of social bonds

Tightening of the environment can occur when a state that is desperate to retain power and control moves towards nationalist authoritarianism that predicates itself on some form of idealised identity that glorifies its history and extolls its values and superiority. It is dependent on a rigid sense of inside (the nation) and outside, and what Fuchs has characterised as a 'friend—enemy

Table 6.1: Elements of the conducive environment

Description	Disruption	Isolation	Entitlement	Desperation
	Instability or breakdown in structures or systems	Separation from social support	The exercise of privilege without consequence	Reaction to an existential threat
Loosening of social bonds	Declining or complete failure of systems of control	Breakdown in social relationships leaves individuals without trustworthy networks for support and advice	Opportunistic prerogative to act with impunity	Loosening of all physical, social and financial welfare provision for certain individuals or groups
	---------------- Balanced environment-------------			
Tightening of social bonds	Increasingly restrictive systems of control	Over-commitment to a social group leaves a person unable to say no and isolated from wider society and other forms of support	Hierarchical prerogative to operate with impunity	Tightening of control leading to oppression of certain individuals or groups

scheme' in which the outsider is a threat to the security and integrity of the inside.

> The friend–enemy scheme constructs scapegoats, typically minorities, that are presented as society's ills and as the causes of social problems. The inclusive form of the friend enemy scheme argues for the inferiority of the enemy group in order to exploit it, and the exclusive form constructs the enemy as inferior for the purpose of deportation, imprisonment or extermination. (Fuchs, 2018, p 783)

Oppression of minority or opposition groups is a form of tightening in the environment in which these groups live. It creates desperation within those groups but may also be symptomatic of a government or political elite that is desperate to retain power and control.

Conclusion

The conducive environment provides the template (summarised in Table 6.1) by which exploitative spaces can be modelled and then disrupted through the targeted use of interventions. Green, Heys and I have sought to overcome the barriers to understanding exploitation, and by providing a comprehensive, boundaried, conceptual and theoretical overhaul of the term, we have posited a coherent reference point for understanding and responding to the unfair treatment of people within their specific cultural and social milieu. Taken together, a new definition and model of exploitation overcomes existing confusion about the relationship between criminal intent, illegal migration, working conditions and cultural relativity that reify ideological and practical fault lines between interpersonal injuries and global inequalities. I have applied this concept here as a meso-level re-conceptualisation of trafficking and modern slavery as patterns of exploitation that includes both but is defined by neither. Having determined that exploitation involves 'using a position of power or privilege to unfairly benefit at the expense of a disadvantaged person or group', we identified it as comprising of three composite parts: (1) power and privilege, (2) unfair benefit and (3) disadvantage. These must be understood in terms of the contextual mechanisms of disruption, isolation, entitlement and desperation that trigger the tightening or loosening of social bonds within the 'normal environment' and thus allow different patterns of exploitation to emerge, adapt and endure. The active presence of these mechanisms increases the conducivity of any environment to the emergence of exploitation. Identifying the components of these mechanisms in any given context presents opportunities to make interventions to end or mitigate the effects of exploitation and make short- to medium-term predictions for the potential effects of intervention. Having described and explained the concept of the conducive environment I will in the next chapters focus attention and analysis on the dynamic relationships between agents and environments over time.

7

The Circles of Analysis: a complex systems model of trafficking and modern slavery

A system comprises a set of components. These components are organised in such a way as to create a series of mechanisms that produce, through their interaction, an output – namely, a pattern of exploitation. This may be deliberate (which is to say an intended purpose or goal), or it may be the unintended and unexpected outcome that is a product, or consequence, of the system's functioning (McDermott, 2014).

The arrangement of the Circles of Analysis model, set out in this chapter, is an adaptation of Felson and Cohen's Routine Activities theory (Felson and Cohen, 1980). In this new model, the circles represent three complex adaptive systems: the suitable target, the motivated offender and the conducive environment. The model posits human trafficking as a non-linear pattern (Byrne and Callaghan, 2014) that emerges from the interaction between the circles, represented at their intersection. The pattern of exploitation cannot be understood or predicted by examining each of the circles in isolation from each other, nor by seeking linear causal pathways, but as resulting logically from multiple antecedents, interactions and outputs that emerge at the intersections of each circle.

Human trafficking is an emergent pattern of behaviour and events that results from the interaction between suitable targets (victims) for the purpose of exploitation and other agents that are motivated to exploit them. However, the pattern cannot be predicted only from identifying the behaviour and characteristics of the potential victim or the perpetrator but as an aggregate of characteristics of the target as a complex adaptive system, characteristics of the perpetrator as a complex adaptive system and the characteristics of the environment from which they both originate and in which they both exist (Jennings, 2014).

Remember, human beings are themselves, complex adaptive systems. As such, we evolve through interaction with other systems within our environment becoming more and more complex (Pycroft and Bartollas, 2014). Logically, this means that the development and interactions of the victim and the perpetrator in the past have been different but have influenced the pattern of their current states; their knowledge and beliefs about their current context and their interactions with each other and the influences of their shared environment. This means that it will be different again in the future, depending upon the effects of different disturbances within the whole system (context in which the human trafficking is occurring) and the states of the people that interact within the exploitative context and the rules by which they organise themselves.

The context in which they both exist is the state in the evolution of the system at a specific point in time (for example, the recent past or the present). It exists between one stable set of states and another; that is, a past state to the present and on to a future state constantly adapting to changes that effect each subsystem and their interactions.

Suitable targets and motivated perpetrators

Environmental variables shape the way in which a system in the form of a person, group, community or society is organised and operates (Wulczyn et al, 2010). How the system responds to the presence or absence of these variables will depend upon the characteristics of the system itself. As the system adapts its operation to its environment, the system inevitably creates changes to its environment also (Byrne and Callaghan, 2014). Thus, a complex adaptive system maintains itself through an evolutionary process of mutual adaptation.

As well as adapting to, and causing changes within, the environment in which the system exists, it will interact with other systems, either competitively or cooperatively, to achieve its desired outcomes. This requires a certain congruity of goals between systems if they are to cooperate. If there is no congruity of goals the interaction between the systems will become competitive. In these circumstances the dominant system will deflect, neutralise or absorb the subordinate system (Jennings, 2014). Nevertheless, the subordinate system is likely to be attracted towards engagement with the dominant system if there remains a perceived congruence of goals and if the risks of engagement with this system are perceived or experienced as less harmful than engagement with other competing systems (for example, an abusive relationship may still meet some basic needs such as food and shelter – despite the abuse of power within this relationship, disengagement from it may be perceived as more dangerous or costly than remaining).

In the context of human trafficking, a victim may not trust law enforcement and protective agencies to be able to accommodate and protect them. They may deflect the intended protection promised by these agencies, opting to self-protect by absconding or returning to the exploiter. This happened in the domestic servitude case study of Suhail and Zuhaila Amil when despite the abuse she had suffered, Zuhaila signed a document for the police confirming that she was not being abused or put under any pressure.

The congruity of goals between cooperative systems adds to the complexity and the associated difficulties in defining and describing a phenomenon. The congruity of goals does not mean that two systems that cooperate share the same goals, only that there is a synergy between them in so far as each assists the other in attaining their desired outcomes through their interactions.

Victims of trafficking and traffickers and exploiters must therefore share an environment that is conducive to the exploitation. However, not all potential victims in that environment will be targeted for exploitation. The tendency has been to identify those at risk of trafficking and exploitation in terms of vulnerability, and as a result, lists of vulnerability and risks factors abound in policy and guidance documents. Such lists appear to be objective and empirical and are drawn from the histories of survivors of trafficking and different forms of slavery and exploitation. However, the predictive value of these lists of vulnerability and risk factors is negligible as they present among most of the people that are known to law enforcement and protective agencies, which is to say that they are lists of similarities that exist among these people.

There are correlations between these vulnerability factors or characteristics and incidents of trafficking and exploitation, but they are not causal factors, nor are they predictive. The predictive factors are those that are *different* (Byrne and Callaghan, 2014) – those that make a person a more suitable target for certain modes of exploitation by certain perpetrators with particular goals. The predictive factors are those that indicate congruity between the wishes and needs (goals) of the potential victim and those of the exploiter. This congruity is what attracts both suitable target and exploiter to each other and creates the foundation of the victim–exploiter microsystem from which may emerge a pattern of slavery (Jennings, 2014).

Mutual needs and goals: the mechanisms that draw the suitable target and exploiter together

While large-scale cases such as Operation FORT and JOKER/KRONE demonstrate the potential earnings that can be made by organised crime groups (OCGs), more often (and depending on the degrees of organisation), the material gains are more modest and may only be so much as is required to make a living given constraints upon opportunities for legitimate employment and gain (Broad, 2018).

Human motivation is, according to Maslow ([1943] 2014), driven by biological, psychological, emotional and social needs. These needs are the stimuli that drive or inhibit behaviour with the aim of gratifying or satiating the need. The goal state (in which needs are met and stabilised) is what serves to attract motivated perpetrators towards suitable targets for exploitation, and targets are similarly attracted towards exploiters who appear to be able to facilitate the achievement of their own goal state.

Focusing on illegal drugs, Schneider and Schneider (2008) discussed the interface between criminally exploitative enterprises and street gangs, explaining that while these are often conflated, they have discrete roots and motivations. Their analysis highlights relational dynamics that can be identified in other contexts for human trafficking and modern slavery.

Youth and street gangs are attributed to the multiple marginalisations of poor modern youth: being constrained to live in poor housing in ill-serviced neighbourhoods where there is a lack of work and opportunity (Schneider and Schneider, 2008; Fitch, 2009); feelings of hopelessness; neighbourhoods that may be violent and disorganised; and as Miller (2009) argues, for young women, there is the common burden of childcare responsibilities and subordination to men.

The formation of street gangs may occur as a congruence of needs of the young people forming the group; for example, the need for physical safety (protection against being targeted for crime), and affiliation (a sense of identity and belonging). Schneider and Schneider suggest that 'perhaps 10% of impoverished youth join street gangs of some form' and that a percentage become 'energised as "crazy" heroes of these formations' (2008, p 361). This suggests that while gang membership offers affiliation there is also the opportunity to gain kudos and status within such groups (Cottrell-Boyce, 2013, p 200).

Though gang life offers affiliation to marginalised youth, gangs tend also to exist at the margins of society, where activities of the gang revolve around livelihood and socialising and involve such activities as: 'Banter and gossip, their entertainment value raised by drinking beer, smoking dope, sniffing glue, throwing dice – also by consuming the images, music, and dance of transnational celebrity gangstas [sic]' (Schneider and Schneider, 2008, p 361).

However, membership of a gang tends to exacerbate a young person's marginalisation from general society the more they become identified with gangs and anti-social behaviour (Knowsley Council, 2015). This reduces their social environment to the gang context alone, which is more conducive to criminal activity and different forms of exploitation. Here criminal activity maintains the group but also tests loyalty to the group (Densley, 2012); for example, crimes and acts of violence are expected to protect the group, protect their territory and earn respect.

In established groups, a desire to join does not guarantee acceptance into the group but may give rise to congruence of goals. A person wants to join the group and is instructed to commit crime or violence as an initiation rite: the result is that the applicant is granted admission but is then bound to the group who have the power to reject or denounce the applicant to the authorities or rival groups.

Youth and street gangs have a limited life cycle; they have been found to be disorganised (Bennett and Holloway, 2004), lacking stable leadership, which is either absent or at best incipient and related to age (Schneider and Schneider, 2008). They coalesce and dissipate over time. However, they are of value to established OCGs because they represent a pool of malleable labour and entrepreneurial talent in neighbourhoods that are potential market places (Schneider and Schneider, 2008). The OCGs thrive on setting up retail opportunities in the territories of street gangs. The organised drug gangs have the money, resources and apparent lifestyle to which gang-involved youths may aspire. From here emerges another congruence of goals between the drug gang, the street gang and maybe individual members of the street gang and people living in the neighbourhood.

Overt displays of wealth and acts of apparent generosity establish members of drug gangs as romantic Robin Hood-type benefactors supporting their community, members of which are then more likely to collude with the criminality as it becomes a part of the local economy (Shelley, 2010; Densley, 2012), similar to the collusion of *favela* communities with OCGs during COVID-19 lockdown periods described in the previous chapter.

Simultaneously, however, weapons, drugs and other criminal resources are trafficked into neighbourhoods and used by the street gangs who perceive the need for protection and gaining respect. This leads to escalations in violence between and within gangs as struggles for control and dominance emerge. The drug gangs are the dominant power, able to exert control over the street gang to develop markets, with severe penalties for failure. To meet the demands of the drug gang, the street gang must become ever more cynical and ruthless in its recruitment and control of younger or junior members, in increasingly charged contexts.

In each of these examples there is a congruence between the goals of the exploiters and those of the exploited, but it is the exploiters that have the greater power and knowledge to control the relationships and they use this to increase the dependence of the victim upon them.

In a family environment in which crime is necessary or is justified, compliance is not only a means of meeting essential basic physical needs, but also a means of gaining approval and affiliation within the family. In the UK context, empirical data from the scoping study (Murphy et al, 2022) of British nationals illustrates these points. One respondent, a survivor of sexual exploitation and criminal exploitation explained:

> All my family was involved in quite a lot of criminality [when she a child, her parents encouraged to open her bedroom window at night to let men bring stolen goods into the house]. All I had to do was let them in and out. I was 12 and I got paid for it ... there was no fear of gangs in my area, there was no gangs, there was people that I knew, people that I liked, it never felt like exploitation.

In the same study, a professional who worked in an NGO (NGO interviewee 17) observed:

> So, you've got the community-based exploitation which can happen between neighbours, between streets, and that takes all different forms and then it goes ... through the various levels until you get to the real organised crime, the high-profile stuff. So, as far as the people that we work with, I would say that the vast majority will be exploited in the community that they're in, that they already exist in, so you're talking about the vulnerabilities, or the difficulties will be highlighted and then people move in because they take advantage of them. (Barlow and Murphy, forthcoming)

Law enforcement, criminal justice systems and child or vulnerable adult welfare and protective services do not adhere to the same values or goals and can be perceived as a threat to the stability of the family and possibly the community. The victim's needs or goals are congruent with the family or affiliation group's needs and goals, which compete with the needs and goals of the external agencies. Individuals, families and affiliation groups compete through adaptation to the agencies' attempts to intervene through disguised compliance (deception),[1] direct resistance, cooperation with other systems that may be licit or illicit, or by relocating.

Conducive environments

How a stable goal state is achieved will be influenced by the narratives that are adopted by actors to make sense of the world and formulate decisions. In gang-affected communities, children may be exposed to gang members and gang behaviour from a very young age (Densley, 2012). In these contexts, criminal activity or criminal attitudes may be normalised – even aspirational for some youths. Target–exploiter congruence occurs when there are synergetic goals and plausible narratives that influence the formation of the relationship (for example: the person's desire for a better life/the motivated exploiter's offer of opportunities for work abroad; the person's desire for family-like affiliation/ promises of care and protection from the exploiters).

On this basis the person's decision to ally themselves to an exploiter, as Katarina did to JB in Operation PELTIER, even when they are aware that the relationship is inherently dangerous, are rational when understood in relation to the perceived alternatives (Elster, 2001).

Sosa Henkoma, a former gang member and survivor of child criminal exploitation, describes and explains this dynamic most eloquently:

> I never saw myself as a victim until I was 23, and that was even after being told I was a victim [laughs]

---

[1] Disguised compliance refers to a parent or carer giving the appearance of cooperating with child welfare agencies to avoid raising suspicions, to allay professional concerns and ultimately to diffuse professional intervention. This neutralises the authority of the agencies and enables the family system to return to its status quo.

because personally, I grew up with someone every day, doing everything with me, showing me things that I believed my father or my mother were meant to show me, doing a lot for me. When I'm looking for, let's say, security, shelter, all these that parents would give you, when I'm looking for it in social services all the actual legal guardians that I meant to have in that moment in time, I'm not finding it. But these people seem to be the ones providing it. So you then have an illusion that these people are your protectors, these people are your safeguarding, and from then, it's that … Why would you want to leave your safeguard and why would you look at your safeguard is anything else than what they are – safety, protection, loved ones?

But really and truly, it's when you look back at, and think about, everything … Was it a relationship? As a common ground where two people come to the decision? But then in that relationship that you have with them exploiters, do you come to a common ground with them? Or is it a fact of you doing everything for them?

And that's when I realised, I'm doing a lot to the other party and the other party wasn't really doing much for me. And that's when I realised that I was a victim of this relationship and that it was not really a relationship. (Henkoma, 2022)

Human beings are essentially rational actors that make a choice or decision based upon a rapid cost/benefit analysis which is based upon the available information and beliefs of the decision-maker (Elster, 2001), but this assertion must be made with certain caveats. As Hodgson, an economist explains, it is necessary to distinguish between claims that people 'maximise manifest payoffs' and claims that people 'maximise utility' and argues for the need to focus upon the historically and geographically specific features of socio-economic systems. Failure to understand the social and psychological determinants of behaviour makes traditional rational choice theory limited in dealing with the real world (Hodgson, 2012, p 94). Hodgson's caveats offer an opportunity to adapt rational choice theory by incorporating it into a complexity-based explanatory model.

Rational choice, as summarised by Elster, is informed by the available information. In systems terms, this information is an input or stimulus that triggers an action or reaction. Decision-making itself is an action that is the initial part of a process that will result in an output.

The information that is available to the decision-maker may be large in terms of quantity but questionable in terms of quality as the information is invariably incomplete. The decision-maker may be aware of some of the gaps in their knowledge (known unknowns) but equally may be unaware of the absence of relevant information also (unknown unknowns). Therefore, the decision-maker must interpret uncertain and incomplete data but can never have the whole picture, or even a sense of what the whole picture may look like (Byrne and Callaghan, 2014).

To cope with and manage such a state of uncertainty, human beings make decisions based upon this incomplete or limited knowledge, which is then measured and interpreted against the decision-maker's experience. This experience comprises:

• Personal experience (subjective).
• Received experience (communicated through other sources; for example, friends, mainstream news and entertainment media, social media, gossip and rumour).

The decision is defined in part by the goals (outcomes) sought by the decision-maker. As Broad suggests, those that are targeted for exploitation may face an irresolvable dilemma. This is a point of crisis when prior coping strategies are inadequate and the available options, as perceived by the decision-maker, exceed their knowledge and experience. For some this may be the point at which they decide whether to engage in the relationship despite potential risks. The exploiter may be at a similar decision point at which they must decide whether or not to exploit another person, to resolve, gratify or satiate their need. Exploiters that are motivated to target people for trafficking and modern slavery or other forms of exploitation are going through similar decision-making processes to the target but the inherent risk to them is lower and they have a fuller picture and greater experience than the target (Giambetta, 2009).

Under adverse conditions, human decision-making and behaviour tends to lead to immediate and extreme loss aversion: gains and losses are interpreted by the decision-maker based upon their goals or desired outcomes (Jennings, 2014). Consequently, especially when under pressure to act, emotions interfere with the decision-making. If the pressure to act is sufficient, the decision-maker may take the 'least-worst option' or decide that to meet their immediate needs, a risk is worth taking. Human decision-makers face myriad possible outcomes. To make the choice or decision the individual must reduce *all* the possible outcomes to *a sample* of possible outcomes (scenario building). This sample is selected from their own knowledge and experience or on a simplified narrative of how they believe the world should work. As alluded to already, whether a decision is considered risky or harmful (and to whom it may be harmful) is greatly influenced by the previous experiences, values and knowledge of the decision-maker and their capacity to frame, identify and analyse options (Sykes and Matza, 2013; Byrne and Callaghan, 2014; Jennings, 2014). In other words, it is influenced by their current and historic interactions with the environments from which they have come.

Exploiter and suitable target: mutual visibility and accessibility

Much of the available guidance on human trafficking and modern slavery such as the 'Operational Indicators of Trafficking in Human Beings' (International Labour Organization, 2009), and the UNODC Human Trafficking Indicators (United Nations Office on Drugs and Crime) refers to indicators that might be signs or signals that someone is a potential victim of trafficking. The inadequacy of these lists has been discussed but signs and signals can be more usefully differentiated and understood as interactions.

Signals are described by Giambetta (2009) as:

> Any observable features of an agent that are intentionally displayed for the purposes of altering the

probability that the receiver assigns to a certain state of affairs or 'an event'. This event can be anything. The 'features' of an agent that make up a signal can be anything too:

- his body;
- his behaviour;
- his appurtenances.[2]

Signs, on the other hand, are described by Giambetta (2009) as 'the environment that is perceptible and that by being perceived modifies our beliefs about something or someone. They do not require a purposive agent.'

A sign can become a signal once action is taken by the signaller to make it overt (that is, takes deliberate steps to display it because it cannot be taken for granted that signs alone will be noticed). Signs are thus converted to signals when the signaller realises that they must make explicit the meaning of a sign (for example, revealing a tattoo).

A person that is identified as a suitable target may not necessarily be aware of the signs that they emit (for example, an accent or idiolect), until an observer draws attention to it and what it reveals about the speaker. Therefore, many of the signs that are emitted by a person that indicate they may be a suitable target may be unconscious (for example, language, accent, body language). At times sign production can be more deliberate (for example, where they choose to hang out, choice of music and associations). Densley (2012) draws attention to how youths that post music videos of themselves on social media, emit signs that indicate their interests, the type of neighbourhood in which they live, their ethnicity, approximate age and aspirations. These deliberate signs communicate to a non-specific, general audience whereas a signal is intended to communicate specific information to an intended receiver.

For a suitable target and a motivated perpetrator of exploitation to engage in a relationship with each other, they must be identifiable to each other. Signalling theory describes

---

[2]   An accessory or other item associated with a particular activity or style of living.

a pattern of behaviour when two actors are attracted towards each other due to the possible congruity of goals. Both have needs which must be negotiated to establish and manage the relationship, but each have access to different information, knowledge and experience. One or other agent must decide whether to communicate (or signal) that information and also how much of the information to communicate. The receiving agent must decide how to interpret the signal (Connelly et al, 2011) and this interpretation may be based upon the identity of the signaller, their trustworthiness and what potential benefits they offer (Giambetta, 2009).

In an exploitative or criminal relationship signalling theory explains under what conditions a signal can be rationally believed by the receiver when the sender has an interest in merely pretending that something is true (Giambetta, 2009). The predatory exploiter can afford to emit specious signals towards the suitable target, implying opportunity, generosity, protection and affection. The costs to the signaller in this instance are minimal, particularly when compared with the benefits they may receive through engaging the target (receiver of the signal). If the predatory exploiter's signal is rejected by the target, they are no worse off than if they had not signalled in the first place. Similarly, if the signal is discovered to be deceitful, the losses to the exploitative signaller are not significant.

The likelihood of the signal being accepted as reliable by the receiver is enhanced if the signaller is already familiar to them, shares some quality such as identity, social history, culture, values and attitudes and is perceived as trustworthy. In Vietnam, Linh was introduced to the bogus employment agency by a family friend who was being used as a recruiter by the traffickers. A similar tactic was used by the traffickers in Operation FORT.

Case example: Piotr and Operation FORT

Piotr was a Polish bricklayer by trade who was finding it hard to earn a living. In February 2015 he met his friend Dawid who told him if he was looking for work in England he could put him in contact with someone who could help. The following day he was told to meet 'Marek' who told him (as he had told others) he would earn £300 per week of which he would receive half (£150) – the remaining £150 would be used to cover his food and accommodation. His £80 travel ticket would also be deducted once he was earning.

Piotr gave 'Marek' his phone number and he rang Piotr about the collection times. 'Marek' also checked Piotr's ID to confirm he could cross the border. He was collected with another Polish male called 'Janusz'. They travelled across Europe and into Dover where he changed minibuses before arriving in Birmingham.

Piotr was met off the bus by Adam Brzezinski's mother, Ignacy Brzezinski. She paid the bus driver £80 and Piotr waited at the address for Adam who arrived and shortly afterwards another male known to Piotr as 'Maniek' arrived. He and Adam took Piotr to a Polish food shop and selected out of date food and then took him to an address where he slept on the sofa in the lounge bedroom with another Polish man and there were a large number of other men present living at the address.

About two days later Adam came to the house on his own. He took everyone's phone numbers and photographed the Polish ID cards on his phone. He then took two other men to open bank accounts. A couple of days later Adam returned to the address and told Piotr that he would have to pay back the £80 cost of travel as well as the food and travel to and from work, and rent, none of which had previously been said to him.

On the same day Adam then took Piotr and two other men to a bank having told them they needed bank accounts to get paid. Adam acted as the interpreter and gave the address details; the men just signed where they were asked to. The men were then taken to another building on the opposite side of the street, where a Polish-speaking male was to keep control of the bank cards – Piotr was informed that he would not be receiving his.

About three or four days later the three men were taken to an employment agency; they had already been told by Adam that they were to inform the agency that National Insurance (NI) numbers were being arranged for them. At the agency a Polish woman took a copy of the ID card and Piotr was told he would be earning £6.50 per hour and would start at 07:00 a.m. He would be unpacking onions from lorries, cleaning and sorting onions by size and type.

Piotr was registered by the employment agency and sent to work. He worked at the onion-packing warehouse once in about a month; he was driven there and worked from 07:00 a.m. to 04:00 p.m. and then collected at the end of the shift. He should have received £50 for this work but received nothing.

Piotr said: 'Adam would pay people who were working on a Friday evening or Saturday morning. He would make his deductions for transport and so on and pay up to half to those who had paid off their debts. I was not paid any money as I had only worked one day.'

The suitable target that hopes to gain from a relationship with the motivated exploiter has far more to lose by having their signal misinterpreted or rejected. Their willingness or commitment to the relationship may be tested and encouraged through a variety of formal and informal means (Densley, 2012) or communication exchanges between both agents.

Human trafficking as well as exploitation unfold over time. First contact between a suitable target and a motivated exploiter may be in childhood, it may be within the family or it may be in the context of crime-affected communities, thus suitable targets may have been identified by motivated exploiters long before they have progressed to recruitment for trafficking and exploitation. Introduction to an exploiter may have been facilitated by another familiar (peer, family member who may also be criminally connected to the exploiter). First contact can occur online and through social media. Different people will be recruited at different times and for different roles depending on the needs of the motivated exploiter.

In Chapter 3 Paco explains how he can spot potential targets by their signs:

> Workers, they range from White, Black, fat, skinny, young, old, whoever wants to work. They're just out there. They're on the estate, trying to get attention by doing little things. They want to be known, want to be with the big guys. You kind of noticed them as well ... You just approach say 'What, you want to go to the country?' He goes 'Yeah, okay'. 'Cool, you start.'

Paco identifies the young people in their community environments and notices the ones whose goals may be kudos or affiliation and status by association. Paco is seeking to recruit 'workers' to run drugs for him. He knows that potential recruits are easy to find, he already has the status they crave and can afford to send an explicit and unambiguous signal that he can meet their needs. This is a demonstration of the unequal but congruent or synergetic goals.

In the case of the Roma family discussed in Chapter 3, the family share the goals. The boy is trained by his mother in the techniques of begging which also reinforce the family rationales for begging (Ballet et al, 2002), but the situation of a child begging in the streets is a sign to criminals that the child and his family are marginalised and in desperate need. If the parents approach a *Kamatari*, they issue a signal that they are in desperate need, probably in response to a signal by the *Kamatari* or one of their agents that they can alleviate the immediate need of the family.

Sosa Henkoma recognises this in his own recruitment and exploitation by drug gangs.

> When someone is vulnerable, is easier for you to take advantage of the situation and I can only really relate it to me which was [about] family and not having family around and being lost in the world, and trying to fit in and that was a big thing for me. Having that sense of brotherhood and sense of belonging and sense of acceptance, that's what pushed me more into that type of culture.
>
> It's like asking what makes it difficult for someone to leave their family. Because once you built a relationship with someone where you are with them 24/7 and you're with them day in and day out, you build a bond. And that's what most exploiters use, they use that emotional bond, that emotional connection, and once you have that emotional connection, it's like you feel you can't move forward or live without that person, you see what I'm trying to say to you mark especially when, like with me, they was my family so it was like I couldn't leave my family or abandon my

family because then what kind of family member am
I? (Interview, 2023)

Exploitation is potentially the start of a long-term strategy for
material gain. Weak or unreliable workers in the context of
criminal activity may be expelled, eliminated or passed onto or
traded with other criminals who may use the victim for other
purposes (for example, sexual exploitation, domestic servitude or
forced labour). Those that perform well, show resilience and a
tolerance for receiving or exerting violence, and signal reliability
increase a crime group or gang's criminal capital, and the initially
exploited person may progress from exploited to exploiter either
within the crime group or independently.

It is noticeable that neither threats nor violence have been
evidenced as part of the recruitment process in any of the case
studies. Through use of signalling theory in his analysis of gang
recruitment, Densley argues that while gangs have capacity to
use violence in recruitment, they rarely do because they have a
willing pool of volunteers. However, once recruited, violence has
multiple functions: discipline, testing of loyalty and commitment,
and blackmail (Densley, 2012).

When violence is used in the context of trafficking and
modern slavery, it can often be extreme and potentially lethal.
Sosa Henkoma described how violence functions in the context
of drug gangs and is the forced criminal exploitation of children
and vulnerable adults:

> Violence is a big thing – most businesses and that,
> you probably get a warning, but with the criminal
> exploitation you probably gets a bang, a punch to your
> face or even getting cut, getting ironed in your chest,
> numerous things and that's just ... that's your morning.
> That's not you getting fired – that's your warning;
> you getting fired ... You might guess that might just
> get you shot in your ... Yeah, bum cheeks. A lot of
> bum cheeks get shot, a lot of feet too get shot, but
> yeah violence is a very big thing. Especially to keep
> someone under control in a place where violence is
> already introduced, where even the addicts are a risk,

then being in a trap house is a risk, then being on the street is a risk, everything is a risk – you see what I'm trying to say to you? So how can you control someone in a risky environment? It's about applying violence, pressuring them with more violence. (Interview, 2023)

Violence increases compliance and desensitisation: a victim that shows no resistance is less likely to run away from the controllers, the need to use violence diminishes (the permanent threat or potential is sufficient) and the value of the exploited person to the exploiter increases – both in terms of their submission to demands for work but also their exchange value between OCGs (Zimmerman et al, 2006).

Case example: Operation FORT

Piotr described being so hungry that he would go to a church to get food. Brzezinski did not like this as he was aware that someone there had helped people who were controlled by Brzezinski escape in the past.

He described an incident when he and another man were taken by Brzezinski in his car and threatened about escaping or trying to do so. He described Brzezinski being very agitated about 'people escaping' as one man had previously 'escaped' with the help of the Salvation Army.

Piotr recalled how another man, after arriving at their address, being taken away by Brzezinski in a car and returning with black eyes and swollen lips and appearing as if he had been beaten. He said to Piotr and the others 'They beat me up'.

A continuum of complexity

Chapter 3 presented potential exploitation scenarios as the degrees of organisation based upon potential flows of earnings from the child's criminal activity. The diagram depicting three scenarios (Figure 7.1) is reproduced as follows.

In the first degree of organisation the potential victim is acting alone and keeps the earnings from their activities. A potential victim that is engaging in work or activity voluntarily, who

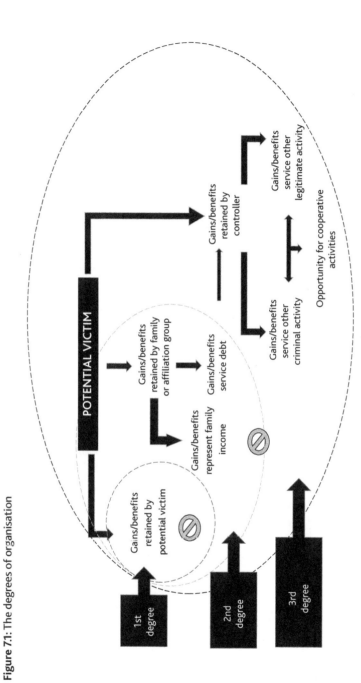

Figure 7.1: The degrees of organisation

POTENTIAL VICTIM

Gains/benefits retained by potential victim

Gains/benefits represent family income

Gains/benefits retained by family or affiliation group

Gains/benefits service debt

Gains/benefits service other criminal activity

Gains/benefits retained by controller

Gains/benefits service other legitimate activity

Opportunity for cooperative activities

1st degree

2nd degree

3rd degree

Source: Barlow and Murphy, forthcoming

gains from the proceeds of their activity is not necessarily being subjected to exploitation through slavery, servitude or forced labour. Their motivation is likely to relate to his or her own physical, emotional, psychological and social needs; for example, food, warmth, shelter, safety, security, affiliation, kudos and even as an act of self-actualisation (Maslow, [1943] 2014). In Operation PELTIER, Hannah and Csilla were acknowledged by the Crown Prosecution Service as being exploited despite the fact that they seemed to have been willing to engage in sex work for their exploiters.

The potential victim's engagement in the work or activity may cause them to be marginalised within society and labelled as delinquent (for example, sex work, begging, extremely low-paid work or unstable piece work) while at the same time increasing their visibility and exposure to criminals. This may also increase their vulnerability to exploitation by predatory others.

Case example: Operation RASTRELLI

When D arrived in London, she began work provided through an escort agency.

In this situation D has decided to earn money to support herself and her family through sex work. She was aware that it is a high-risk occupation, but her circumstances were such that she could see few if any alternative choices available to her. Her calculation was that if she must engage in sex work, she would do so in London where there is a lucrative market for cheap sex and she could earn sufficient to end the work sooner than if she worked in her home country and region. She was seeking to maximise the utility of her decision.

Each intersection is an emergent micro-state. In this model the biographical histories of the actors are as important as geographical locations, as these promote, or inhibit, the patterns of behaviour that occur during the interactions.

For D, London as a conducive environment offered the availability of customers seeking sexual services. This was an attractor for D to that environment creating a possibility space, in which there is a congruity of goals or needs between both D and potential customers.

The pattern of sex work in this scenario is the stable possibility space, in which the motivated sex worker's needs are met. This possibility space will likely destabilise as disturbances occur in any of the micro-states. The pattern of behaviour will then cease (as it is no longer functional to goal achievement) or adapt in response to the new stimuli, such as law enforcement activity, relocation of customer base, increased competition or new opportunities.

This first scenario essentially describes a pattern of illicit work activity by D. It is neither very sophisticated in its organisation nor complex in its goals. By following the pathway of the earnings from her sex work, it can be established that at this stage it was unlikely to be an output of forced sexual exploitation. However, she is in a risky environment where she is vulnerable to abuse by customers and to exploitation by criminal predators. It is the congruence of these goals that causes the interaction in a conducive environment in which all actors exist at the same time and are configured in the diagram (Figure 7.2) as follows.

In the next scenario, there are changes in each of the micro-states as D transitions from being in control of her work and selecting her suitable customers to becoming a suitable target for other motivated perpetrators of sexual exploitation.

Another woman with whom D had become acquainted told her of somewhere she could stay and keep more of her money. This was appealing to D and so she was introduced to 'John' and 'Sylvia' who were also Romanian. She was not aware that the couple controlled several brothels in south-east London. When she moved in, Sylvia put D's passport and other documents in a safe. Very quickly John made advances on D and so began a brief sexual relationship. When D told him that she did not want to continue having sex with him he violently beat and raped her. From that point she was forced to work as a prostitute for 'John' and 'Sylvia' and was frequently moved between properties and forced to take customers throughout the day and night, seven days a week.

D's earnings are retained by 'John' and 'Sylvia'. The Circles of Analysis may then be configured as in the diagram (Figure 7.3) as follows. Note that the child is now the suitable target, and the motivated exploiter is the child's parent or another family member. The conducive environment circle remains unchanged.

Figure 7.2: The Circles of Analysis configured to represent D and her pattern of illicit sex work

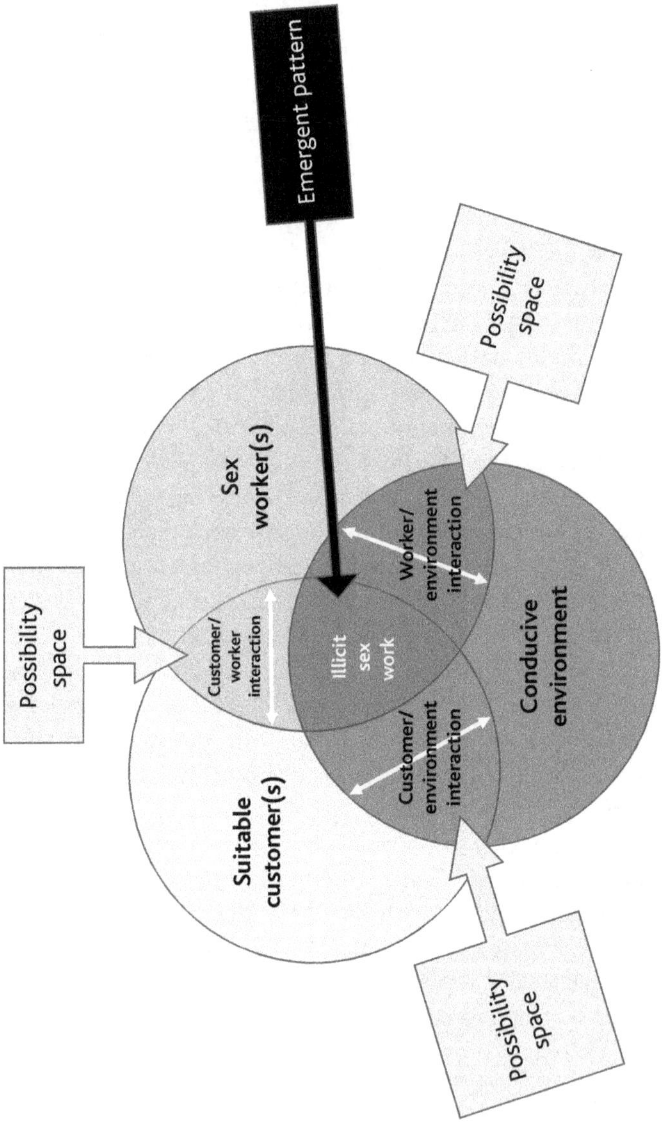

Figure 7.3: Configuration with D as suitable target for external motivated perpetrator(s)

Emergent pattern

Possibility space

Possibility space

possibility space

Motivated perpetrators (Jon and Sylvia)

Suitable target (D)

Conducive environment

Forced sex work

Target/ perpetrator interaction

Perpetrator/ environment interaction

Target/ environment interaction

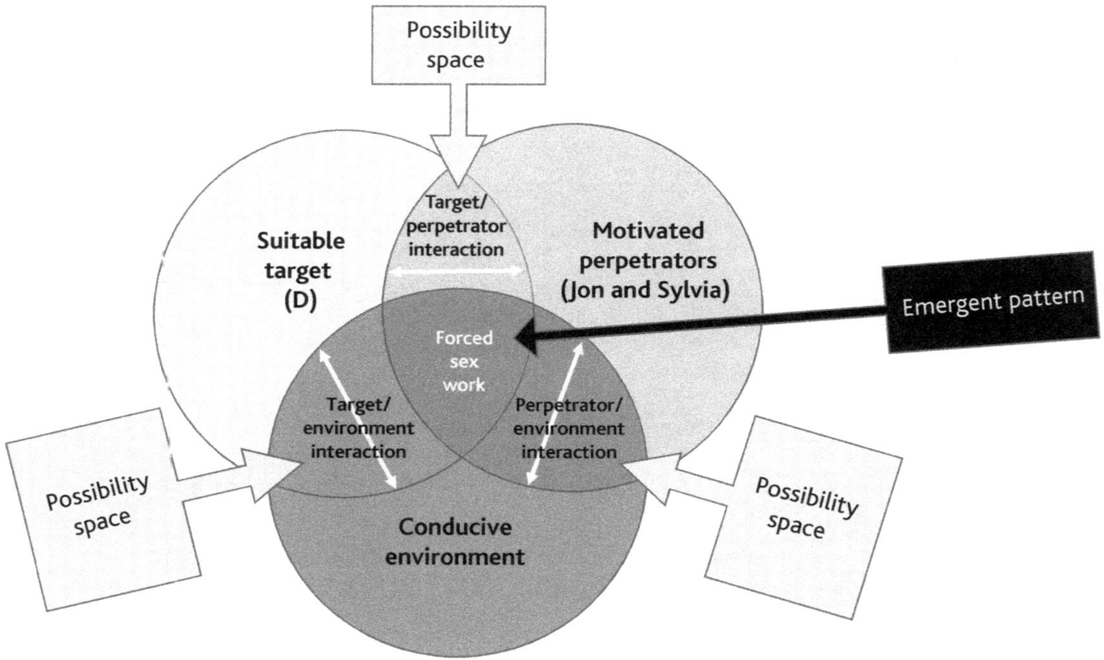

Again, the pathway of the earnings is significant and goes some way to offering insight into the exploiters' motivation. D's earnings are retained by 'John' and 'Sylvia'. They have trapped D into their business which includes several brothels. Their operation is sophisticated and well organised. They have recruited D through another woman that they were controlling, deceived her, ensnared her, isolated her and increased her dependence upon them until they had complete control of her.

When D was recruited, the young woman who introduced her to 'John' and 'Sylvia' knew what D's goals were. She made the invitation with knowledge of 'John' and 'Sylvia's' business that D did not have. 'John' and 'Sylvia' welcomed D but immediately took control of her ID documents and earnings, taking advantage of her naivety. The needs of the perpetrator and target in this scenario are obviously congruent but it is 'John' and 'Sylvia' who have the greater knowledge and experience. 'John' grooms D into what she thinks is a romantic relationship, rather like JB's initial relationship with Anna in Operation PELTIER.

John's violent assault and multiple rape of D is not simply an act of anger when she rejected him as a lover – the violence was functional, intended to dominate her, make her submit and show what can happen when she is non-compliant. As Sosa explained, 'How can you control someone in a risky environment? It's about applying violence, pressuring them with more violence.'

The pattern of sexual exploitation through forced sex work is the stable macro-state that has emerged from the interactions of the micro-states. This will likely destabilise over time. D's earning potential through this pattern will diminish. This may also destabilise the perpetrator/target micro-state as she becomes less to meet 'John' and 'Sylvia's' needs in terms of attaining their goals. To maintain the income the system will need to adapt. This may result in a reorganisation of the system. Sylvia may offer D a way to reduce her burden of work by recruiting others to work for 'Sylvia' and 'John' as she had been recruited. She may be used for other work such as housework, working on reception or traded as Anna was in Operation PELTIER.

In the earlier example of Suhail and Zuhaila Alim, the stable pattern that emerged from the three dynamic micro-states was one of exploitation through domestic servitude. In this case, the exploitation was contained within the family who were the beneficiaries of the victim's labours. It was well planned and maintained over a significant period and might be considered to exhibit the characteristics of the second degree of organisation.

In Operation FORT and in Operation JOKER/KRONE, described in Chapter 3, the work earnings of the victims are used to facilitate and fund other criminal or legitimate businesses or cooperative enterprises with other criminals or crime groups and illustrate how victims can transition between safety and vulnerability, from one exploitative situation to re-victimisation in other situations.

The following diagram (Figure 7.4) illustrates this continuum of complexity and takes as a case example that of the Roma boy and his family described in Chapter 3.

In this scenario the child and their family are victims of the motivated offender. The example is complex in terms of its dynamics and the relationships between multiple systems, but the model helps to differentiate victims from perpetrators and also identifies those who may occupy a dual role of victim and perpetrator. This is an important set of distinctions. I shall illustrate the emerging options for practitioners by referring back to the example of the Roma boy. The boy is exploited by his parents in order to service a debt to the *Kamatari*. This is because the parents are forced to make their child beg under threat of penalty. Although they are causing their son to beg, the flow of earnings leads back to the *Kamatari*, and practitioners have the benefit of existing legislation to intervene to protect the child (Children Act 1989, s 47), to choose to not prosecute the parents (Modern Slavery Act 2015, s 45) but to investigate and prosecute the controllers in relation to exploitation, including exploitation of a child (Modern Slavery Act 2015, ss 2, 3, 3(6)).

Conclusion

The Circles of Analysis theory provides a multi-dimensional model of human trafficking, modern slavery and exploitation. The benefit of the model is its transferability between disciplines and professions that will enable professionals to structure their investigations, assessments and interventions

Figure 7.4: The continuum of complexity: from simple, disorganised crime as a minimal enterprise to organised crime as a major enterprise (representing the criminal exploitation of Roma children in Operation GOLF)

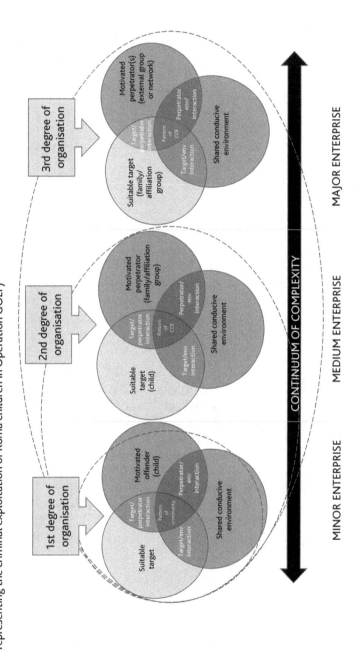

(Pycroft and Bartollas, 2014). It offers a richer, holistic analysis of trafficking and modern slavery as a dynamic process of non-linear development over time (Byrne and Callaghan, 2014) which is superior to the current reductive, descriptive models that have been used to inform policy and practice (Hassett and Stevens, 2014).

Understanding the temporal and developmental dimensions of exploitation enables organisations and practitioners to formulate primary interventions to address the needs of victims and the motivations of potential exploiters who increase their vulnerability to exploitation or transition to exploitative behaviour and roles. It informs secondary interventions that seek to intervene to safeguard people that have been exploited, and thus prevent re-victimisation or transition to exploiter, supporting them towards safety and recovery and identifying opportunities for law enforcement to disrupt the operations of traffickers and exploiters. Finally, the model supports tertiary interventions by offering useful lines of criminal investigation and prosecution strategies (Barlow, 2019).

The Circles of Analysis model should provide a theoretical foundation for an empirically informed approach to systemic investigation, protection and prosecution strategies that structure, not replace, professional judgement and decision-making, providing a framework within which professionals can organise, interpret and present the complex evidence that may lead them towards, or away from, the identification of actual and potential cases of trafficking and modern slavery (Hart et al, 2003; Byrne and Callaghan, 2014; Pycroft and Bartollas, 2014). Such a framework is the subject of the next chapter.

8

Conclusion

Academic and policy responses to the problem of human trafficking and modern slavery have largely failed to help frontline professionals in identifying potential victims. This is due to flawed assumptions about the people that are targeted, the perpetrators and the processes of the exploitation. Consequently, understanding of the problem to date has been reductive, and current interventions to prevent exploitation, pursue traffickers and the beneficiaries of modern slavery and support victims towards safety and recovery, are limited (Barlow, 2022; Murphy et al, 2022). Much of the available literature in the field has focused on the trafficking of women and girls. Existing research has also tended to focus upon characteristics of victims and the impact of trafficking and exploitation upon the physical and mental health of victims. This victim-centred attention in the research has contributed little other than to describe the nature and scope of this form of abuse.

Most attention has been paid to the characteristics of those targeted for exploitation and where they have come from, so that knowledge of traffickers and exploiters is often cited as a gap in our understanding of these problems (Rudd, 2017). In fact, the gap is not so much a lack of knowledge or understanding of traffickers, but rather the aetiology and dynamics of trafficking and exploitation as a result of the interactions between targeted victim, perpetrator and their shared environments.

Relevance of this model and research

Current responses to the problem of human trafficking and modern slavery are predicated upon identification, investigation and prosecution, and so appear to be rooted in criminal justice approaches to the abuse and exploitation of vulnerable groups (Moore, 1995). The criminal justice approach emphasises the identification of a crime, it views the motivations of the criminal as an important cause of the crime and responds to this through the imposition of sanctions. As such it is a largely reactive approach.

By contrast, safeguarding models in health and social care tend to situate the problem with the victim and their family, and adopt an alternative approach that emphasises prevention through the identification and reduction of 'risk factors', such as vulnerability and adversity, a target-hardening approach that emphasises building a protective environment and strengthening resilience.

The criminal justice system and the health and social care system share a common concern that is abuse and exploitation through human trafficking and modern slavery but they perceive the results differently: the criminal justice system identifies a criminal event; the safeguarding community identifies harm experienced by the complainant – the victim (adapted from Moore, 1995). There is a gulf between the concepts, principles, practice and values of the two approaches. Both can be equally reductive in terms of their explanation of causes of trafficking and modern slavery. However, attempts to respond to human trafficking for all forms of exploitation reflect the dominance of the criminal justice approach in both policy and practice, which emphasises the need to respond to the problem as a crime first and a health and safeguarding issue second.

Proper identification of human trafficking, modern slavery and other forms of exploitation can only occur if we are sensitised to look for something and recognise it as worthy of investigation. Investigation involves the seeking, finding and interpreting evidence that leads towards or away from a hypothesis for what has happened. The interpretation of the evidence is dependent upon theory. If trafficking and modern slavery is conceptualised in terms of crime and perpetrator first and foremost, with only a secondary concern for the victim impact we distort and bias our understanding of the event and limit the range of responses. Similarly, if we only conceptualise the problem in terms of the vulnerability of potential victims and the harm that has been or is likely to be suffered, we fail to understand the relationships of potential and actual victims with the perpetrators of the abuse and the processes involved. A theory enables us to develop a narrative to describe events and experiences by informing the relevant questions that drive the inquiry, organise evidence and make pragmatic, informed decisions and plans.

My research, that informs this book, has produced a new and innovative unifying theory that meets the needs of both the criminal justice system and the health and social care system. As a unifying theory it provides common ground for practitioners from across disciplines, upon which they can organise and present evidence, discuss and analyse problems, and jointly formulate and share interventions that are proportionate to the needs and rights of victims of trafficking and modern slavery and represent social justice for those who are not only victims but also may have transitioned into similarly abusive and exploitative roles.

The Circles of Analysis as an aetiological construction of trafficking and modern slavery

Human trafficking and modern slavery, as a phenomenon, has defied a neat and clear definition and description. Consequently, empirically informed theory has been difficult to find. Efforts to develop theory that explains human trafficking and forms of exploitation have been rather like the top-down taxonomical approach to behavioural profiling of violent criminals developed by the US's FBI (Woodiwiss, 2004). This is exemplified by the UK Government's 'County Lines Guidance' (Her Majesty's Government, 2017), and the typology of 17 types of modern slavery offences (Cooper et al, 2017), the ILO Operational Indicators of Trafficking and the UNODC Trafficking Indicators. The reality is that people's experiences of trafficking, slavery, servitude, forced labour and exploitation, varies in terms of the aetiology of their involvement and relationships with other potentially suitable targets, with the perpetrators of their exploitation, and their interactions with the environments from which they and the perpetrators emerge.

The contextual safeguarding approach (Firmin, 2017) has made a considerable contribution in developing a more systemic framing of the problem of extra-familial child abuse and exploitation in the UK but does not provide a theory for the phenomenon itself. With the contextual safeguarding approach, Firmin has, however, established the need to understand the child, their behaviour, activities and decision-making in the context of their environment and lived experiences. The approach integrates Bourdieu's Social theory (1986) with Felson and Cohen's Routine Activities/Lifestyles (Felson and Cohen, 1980) theory and principles of situational crime prevention. This is a more 'bottom-up' approach that emphasises the characteristics and motivations of the child and their environment. However, as a safeguarding model, it omits an important control parameter for abuse and exploitation; namely, the presence, characteristics and motivations of the abuser and the nature of the abusive relationship.

The Circles of Analysis is a theory that explains trafficking and exploitation of both children and adults in an evolutionary, adaptive and emergent way, making it possible to recognise (and set out evidentially) how and why a person is being trafficked and exploited presently and their risk for future re-victimisation.

Therefore, descriptive terminology that refers to a possible output of a system should not be the starting point for tactical and strategic decision-making ('If trafficking ... then ...'). Instead, the foundation of decision-making should be understanding human trafficking and modern slavery as an output of a complex of systems (namely, the victim as a suitable target, the perpetrator and the conducive environment), which are maintained by a range of mechanisms over time. These principles are the keystone of the Circles of Analysis model which describes and explains trafficking of human beings and exploitation and offers a new theoretical framework for structured professional judgement and decision-making. The complete model is set out in Figures 8.1–8.3 as follows.

With the theoretical foundations established, I will turn to the questions that I asked at the beginning of this book.

Figure 8.1: The Circles of Analysis: control parameters and possibility spaces

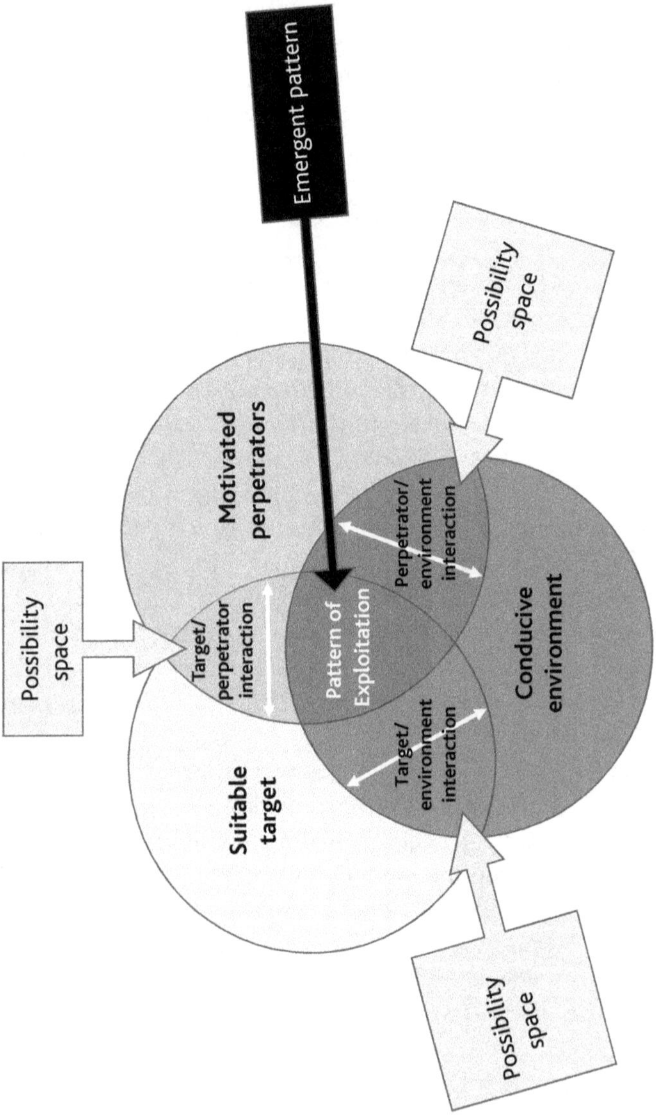

Figure 8.2: The degrees of organisation

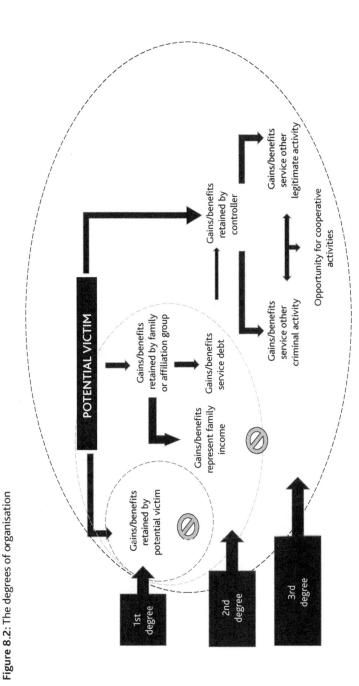

Source: Barlow and Murphy, forthcoming

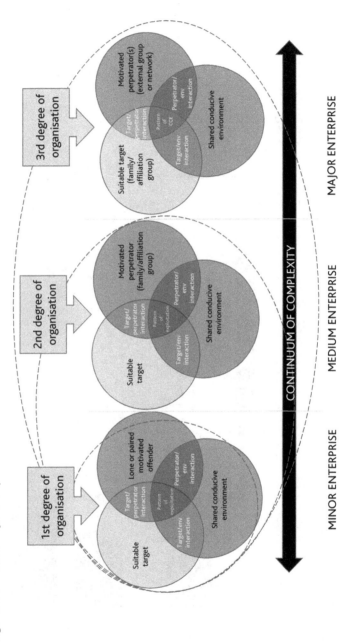

Figure 8.3: The continuum of complexity: depicting child criminal exploitation from simple (linear) crime as a minimal enterprise to organised crime as a major enterprise

(1) What are the components and mechanisms that maintain the relationships between the victim, their environment and the perpetrators that lead to human trafficking and modern slavery?

The Circles of Analysis model provides a theoretical explanation of the relational contexts to human trafficking, modern slavery, slavery-like practices and other forms of abuse and exploitation. In summary, it achieves this by:

(a) Differentiating between the potential victim as a suitable target, the motivated offenders and the conducive environments from which they both emerge.

(b) Understanding each circle as a complex system with a past state, present state and future state. The future state can be plausibly estimated from the patterns of past and present states based upon the interactions between each system.

(c) Analysing each circle as control parameters for the emergent relationship: the characteristics of the suitable target/victim and the perpetrators, and the conduciveness of the environment to abuse and exploitation, all determine the patterns of behaviour and adaptation over time.

(d) Identifying the intersection point (the overlap in the Venn diagram) which represents the 'possibility space' in which the shared goals and interactions between the three systems create and maintain the present space: the opportunity for exploitation to emerge as an identifiable pattern.

The method for testing this as a worthwhile (that is, useful) construct for practitioners in different disciplines was achieved through the novel use of focus group interviews. The focus group method as it was applied in developing this model, was innovative as an approach to complexity research, which usually relies on case study data rather than qualitative interviews (Gear, Eppel, and Koziol-Mclain, 2018). Initially conceived as a method for gaining 'product feedback' on the Circles of Analysis model, the method proved well suited to a process of collaborative refinement of the model, combining the knowledge and experience of myself as the researcher and the participants as equals (Griffith, Griffith, and Slovik, 1990). This collaborative approach confirmed the potential of the Circles of Analysis as a framework for the formulation of interventions that are proportionate to the nature and organisation of the abuse and exploitation (for example, whether a welfare intervention would be more appropriate, proportionate and effective than a criminal justice intervention).

(2) Precisely how can the relational understanding of trafficking of human beings, modern slavery, servitude, forced or compulsory labour and other forms of e exploitation proposed in this book result in better strategic and tactical responses by organisations concerned with safeguarding victims, and pursuing and prosecuting traffickers and perpetrators of modern slavery and exploitation?

The refinements proposed by colleagues and professionals from law enforcement, justice systems, statutory safeguarding agencies and third-sector organisations are helpful in the ongoing development and application of this model. It is also supported in criminological theory by Anna Sergi's work on organised crime and mafia. In her recent analysis of policing models in combatting organised crime, Sergi (2017) differentiates between 'ordinary' organised crime and mafia organised crime as a spectrum of organisation, social embedding, history and culture. She demonstrates the interaction between institutional understanding of the criminal threats and historical events that have shaped these perceptions.

By incorporating historical and environmental considerations, this spectrum structure offers a developmental or evolutionary model of organised crime. Taking the suggestions of other academics and practitioners and synthesising these with Sergi's concept enabled me to refine and improve the 'degrees of organisation' and the 'continuum of complexity' sections in the Circles of Analysis. These refinements to the Circles of Analysis model would also appear to extend Sergi's spectrum from lone criminality or disorganised crime as a potential evolutionary point towards involvement in, or connection to, highly structured organised crime.

More importantly though, the graphic representation of these degrees of organisation and complexity highlight the extremely dangerous and precarious position of individuals, families or affiliation groups that are controlled by the major enterprise organised crime groups, and explains how a suitable target for exploitation can occupy the role of victim and perpetrator simultaneously, or transition from victim to perpetrator.

When the relational possibility space becomes clear, a range of preventive, protective, disruptive and criminal justice opportunities emerge. These opportunities are potentially mutually beneficial and reinforcing. Crucially, the understanding of both historic and current conditional factors can be used to formulate plausible scenarios that are likely to occur as a result of intervention, enabling the whole safeguarding system to pre-empt adaptations by the criminal system and plan for them. If this model is shared across agencies, there is far greater potential for harmonisation of procedures, and consistency in responses to human trafficking and modern slavery.

(3) How can a theoretical model for understanding of trafficking and modern slavery be applied across different professional disciplines and different exploitation contexts?

In this book, I have demonstrated that knowledge of instrumental and expressed violence, theories of organised crime and routine activities and rational choice theory all offer important insights into abuse and exploitation. Similarly, public protection theory and practice has benefitted greatly from ecological systems theory but at the same time, protection protocols have followed similar 'top-down' logic to that which is applied by law enforcement and criminal justice approaches to general crime. Surprisingly, there remains a lack of focus on the perpetrators of the abuse and on the relationship dynamics between perpetrator and target. This is a significant gap in current systemic approaches.

To overcome this problem, the Circles of Analysis model has applied the principles of complexity theory to combine the ecological principles of standard systemic practice; certain criminological theories such as routine activities, rational choice and situational crime prevention; and theories of organised crime. It has thereby been able to build upon the strengths of current approaches but also reach past their limitations in relation to understanding human trafficking, modern slavery and other forms of exploitation and developing new theory (Kalmar and Sternberg, 1988). The Circles of Analysis model is a theoretical framework that enables an emergent, constructivist ('bottom-up') approach to identifying, analysing, and understanding patterns of human trafficking, modern slavery and exploitation. As such, it is not tied to the legislation, policies or procedures of any single state or agency and can be applied in any social, economic, political or cultural context (Malangone, 2018). This is because the environment of the potential victim and the traffickers represents one of the three control parameters for the functioning of the system that creates an output of exploitation. Therefore, the phenomenon cannot be understood without fully considering the social, economic, political and cultural history and current conditions of the environment from which the pattern of exploitation emerges. For this reason, it is transferable to any jurisdiction.

The context of the original thesis (Barlow, 2019) was child criminal exploitation (CCE), but in collaborating with other professionals through informal interviews and the formal, semi-structured focus groups, it became apparent that the Circles of Analysis model is likely to be transferable to other contexts of abuse and exploitation. Professionals have also applied the model in developing responses to domestic abuse, as well as intra-familial and extra-familial child abuse.

Since completion of the original research, the model has been applied to serious and organised crime in seminar discussions and lectures with postgraduate students studying modern slavery and organised crime at St Mary's University, as a model for analysing and describing organised crime in fragile and insecure environments, presented and discussed at international academic conferences and knowledge exchange events across Europe.

So, feedback indicates that the model is transferable to other contexts, but further work may be required to validate such applications. In particular the 'degrees of organisation' and the 'continuum of complexity' sections may need some adaptation in order to be applied outside of the context of trafficking of human beings, exploitation, modern slavery and forced labour.

Other emergent themes

While this thesis is concerned with criminal exploitation of children, the research has inevitably required comparison with other contexts of child abuse and exploitation as well as the wider context of trafficking of human beings and modern or contemporary slavery. The research has included examination of professional and academic literature, and formal and informal interviews and discussions with practitioners and fellow academics (at conferences, seminars, symposia and other colloquia). All of these inputs have informed the development of the Circles of Analysis model from which a range of relevant themes have emerged that are worthy of some consideration here.

Confusions and conflations

Recorded cases of criminal exploitation have involved children and adults that have been coerced into crimes (such as ATM theft, pickpocketing, bag snatching, counterfeit DVD selling, cannabis cultivation, metal theft, benefit fraud and sham marriages), as well as being forced to beg (ECPAT UK, 2010). However, in the time since commencing this thesis, the county lines model of illicit drugs dealing in the UK has come to dominate the professional, academic, political and public discourse on criminal exploitation of children and, to some extent, the targeting of vulnerable adults for the take-over of their homes (a pattern of intimidation and exploitation known as 'cuckooing'). The county lines phenomenon has almost displaced child sexual exploitation (CSE) as a source of public and political anxiety and often seems to be conflated with the problems of youth violence and knife crime in England and Wales.

It is not surprising then, that so many conflations and confusions arise because the reality is that CCE, CSE, knife crime and peer-on-peer youth violence (and by extension early and forced marriage, female genital mutilation and radicalisation) are all manifestations of exploitation that are patterns of violence towards children.

These patterns are maintained by a number of instrumental abuses including sexual abuse, physical abuse, psychological abuse and neglect but the current focus upon specific types of exploitation and legal arguments over the definition of trafficking, slavery, who is or is not a victim or perpetrator of trafficking and slavery, has created a narrow perception of what trafficking and modern slavery may include or even what it looks like.

Although there has been a lack of research and data specifically focusing on traffickers and exploiters, much of the literature in the field refers to the high levels of violence and psychological abuse that are used to coerce and control victims to make them engage in the exploitative activity. Therefore, the problem of trafficking and modern slavery has been reframed in this thesis as a problem of abuse which enables exploitation. This was an important first step in developing a theoretical model and is essential in describing, explaining and understanding all forms of exploitation. Understood in this way, the nature of a person's vulnerability to victimisation or re-victimisation is better understood as an integral component in their development and lived experience. This is supported, in theory, by Finkelhor's concept of 'developmental victimisation' and Felitti's concept of adverse childhood experiences and their traumagenic dynamic effects on lifelong health and development (Felitti et al, 1998). The assumption of linear causal pathways that underpin most policy and procedural responses to human trafficking and modern slavery, and the 'top-down' taxonomical description of the phenomenon, has been based on aspects of similarity to identify the possible presence of exploitation. A range of risk assessment and management protocols has interpreted these correlations between cases of modern slavery as markers for exploitation, leading to a further conflation of risk. This leads to several problems in terms of identification of human trafficking and modern slavery, understanding of those targeted for exploitation and the motivations and criminogenic needs of perpetrators and human facilitators of the exploitation.

Risk assessment and vulnerability

Exploration of literature in the field of trafficking of human beings, modern slavery, labour exploitation and criminal exploitation revealed a limited amount of existing academic research outside of sexual exploitation. That which exists often repeated the same conclusions but offered very little insight into the problem, often focusing on specific issues (within what is actually a diverse and far-reaching phenomenon) such as children going missing from home (Shipton, Setter, and Holmes, 2016), exploitation of children and vulnerable adults' drug production and dealing operations (Pitts, 2007; Robinson, McLean, and Densley, 2018; Whitaker et al, 2018; Harding, 2020) or providing overviews of the nature and extent of the problem (Brotherton and Waters, 2013; Setter and Baker, 2018). These contributions have in varying degrees helped to identify types and scope of exploitation and some have stressed the importance of recognising the intersection between modern slavery, servitude and forced or compulsory labour and other forms of abuse and exploitation (Setter and Baker, 2018). However, there is a pervasive tendency in all these reports to adopt the language of risk and then focus upon the victim's vulnerability, neglecting the victim's agency and relationships with and to their exploiters (O'Connell Davidson, 2016; Heys, 2023).

The use of risk terminology in describing and defining exploitation is potentially problematic as the application of the language of risk is rarely attached to any formal risk theory. For instance, Hart et al (2003) set out two common approaches to risk assessment thus:

- Professional Judgement which comprises at least three different procedures: unstructured professional judgement (also sometimes known as unaided clinical judgement); anamnestic risk assessment which imposes a limited degree of structure on the assessment process; structured professional judgement.
- Actuarial Approaches to Risk (of which there are two types): the actuarial use of psychological tests or the use of actuarial risk assessment instruments (also known as tools, tests or aids).

The development and use of systematic risk-assessment models has enjoyed increasing popularity but relatively few tools are empirically based (Lyons, Doueck, and Wodarski, 1996) or adequately tested in terms of outcomes and unintended effects, particularly for children (Barlow, Fisher, and Jones, 2012).

'At risk' can become a non-specific term that is used interchangeably with vulnerability, and this ambiguous language has undermined risk assessment, management and investigation of trafficking and modern slavery at all levels, from practice to policy. 'Risk' refers to a hazard that is incompletely understood and by its nature will inevitably be uncertain depending on the characteristics of the hazard (for example, the likelihood that it will occur, the frequency with which it will occur, the seriousness of the consequences and the imminence of the hazardous event). Furthermore, these multiple facets are all context-specific (Hart, Kropp, and Laws, 2003).

Counter-trafficking and safeguarding protocols do not reflect this complexity. There has been a tendency to provide practitioners with checklists of 'risk factors' and until recently to weight these risk factors numerically (Jay, 2014), offering a dubious credibility of pseudo-science to risk-management protocols: the numbers are meaningless and the 'risk factors' have little or no predictive value as they are no more than correlates with CCE or any other form of exploitation. To effectively assess risk, to intervene to prevent victimisation or re-victimisation, disrupt or stop perpetrators, practitioners need to be able to gather information about people and circumstances. If they are to make decisions regarding the nature and likely consequences of potential exploitation, the needs and resources of the target, the motivations and capabilities of the perpetrators and the contexts in which exploitation may occur, this information must come from multiple sources and various lines of enquiry (Hart, Kropp, and Laws, 2003; Barlow, Fisher, and Jones, 2012).

The task for professionals in each of their fields is not to predict whether a suitable target is going to be exploited and then respond. Such predictions are meaningless without fuller discussion of the nature, imminence, severity and frequency of the abuse and exploitation to which the potential victim may be subjected or which the perpetrator is likely to apply (Hart, Kropp, and Laws, 2003). This process of evaluation requires assessors or investigators to be able to make sense of how and why a person may have been abused or exploited in the past, as well as how and why a perpetrator has come to abuse a child or other person in the past (historic conditional factors). Historical conditional factors offer insights into how these past experiences are likely to have influenced their current choices and decisions under the present conditions in which they are made (current conditional factors). This helps assessors and investigators anticipate the effects of new inputs (triggers) to the system and formulate realistic scenarios for future actions and reactions (current consequential factors) (Barlow, 2017). Rather than prediction of harm occurring, this process enables assessors to estimate the most plausible scenarios in which harm is most likely to occur and then formulate plans to reduce the likelihood and/or the harmful impact of these.

The complexity of the configuration of these multiple facets of the suitable target, the perpetrator and their environments means that traditional actuarial approaches to assessment of risk cannot be applied as there are too few fixed variables. The information available to professionals tasked with responding to such cases is often incomplete, inaccurate and often incomprehensible, rendering professional judgement and decision-making a formidable task. The lack of any theoretical underpinning to the risk assessment and management protocols means that such lists and flow-chart approaches to the problem are defined and applied by the knowledge and traditions of the agency or practitioner that are applying them. This causes inconsistency of approach and prioritisation, leading to inter-disciplinary tensions and miscommunication.

Problems of definition and identification

As Hart et al (2003) explain, a hazard must be defined in order to be discussed and studied clearly. Human trafficking and modern slavery and exploitation have proven to be stubbornly resistant to formal and widely agreed definitions. It is not possible to provide a completely precise unambiguous, cast-iron definition of modern slavery and exploitation, so the definition of exploitation within conducive environments proposed by Simon Green, Alicia Heys and I may itself be challenged and definitions may need revision as patterns evolve.

There are many difficulties that investigators, safeguarding professionals and lawyers face in identifying exploitation and presenting evidence for criminal exploitation. The Haughey review of the Modern Slavery Act 2015 (2016) represented the evolution of understanding, responses and current practices by all agencies to the problem (of modern slavery) but is also a useful measure of the extent to which understanding is limited, and cross-agency responses lack theoretical foundations. This is reflected in the contributions of participants in the focus groups conducted as part of my original research to develop the Circles of Analysis model. Consequently, tactical and strategic responses have tended to be limited in their response and reductive in their analysis.

At national and international levels, treaties, conventions, protocols and legislation follow assumptions of linear causality of trafficking and modern slavery, thereby underpinning the proliferation of checklist procedures to identify cases and the flow-chart decision-making protocols that accompany them. The unhelpful nature of these policies and procedures is compounded by the downward pressure on frontline professionals and first responders in social work, law enforcement, border control, education and health services, as policy makers call for frontline professionals to be more accountable for children and vulnerable adults becoming entrapped in gangs, organised crime, exploitation, sexual exploitation and radicalisation.[1] The punitive political attitude towards professionals tasked with combatting the exploitation has suggested that identifying victims is a matter of 'common sense', and failure to respond robustly to cases of exploitation is an act of wilful neglect (Stevenson, 2015). Such criticism and pressure may be unfair when there is nothing available that enables professionals to make difficult, nuanced decisions and instigate proportionate interventions that respect human rights, nor anything that helps an agency to keep a vulnerable person safe; there is nothing currently that reflects the reality of the cases that they are trying to work with. No doubt there is sometimes bad practice, but bad practice is sometimes a symptom of professional defensiveness, lack of training, professional supervision and support, lack of resources or the 'silo effect'.

The focus groups that contributed to the development of the Circles of Analysis model were made up of 29 professionals. These

---

[1]   At the time of writing the latest example of this relates to knife crime. See also Stevenson (2015).

professional participants had a strong, enthusiastic commitment to the protection of children and vulnerable adults, to the prevention of abuse and re-victimisation, and to the disruption, arrest and prosecution of offenders. The collective knowledge and expertise of the participants was extensive, and it was notable that they shared many common frustrations, not least of which was the pressure upon them to stop vulnerable people being exploited. They felt constrained by inadequate and inappropriate assessment and investigation protocols which did not help them unravel the complexity of the cases they were managing.

Previously, similar frustrations have been highlighted elsewhere: Baroness Alexis Jay (2014) recorded frustrations by practitioners in the specialist CSE team in Rotherham who explained that the numeric risk-assessment protocol they were required to use did not accurately capture the nature of the risk to some children, often underestimating it because of the type of evidence that it relied upon. A similar problem was also identified by Barlow, Fisher, and Jones (2012) in their systematic review of assessment tools in child and family social work. In my own work developing a systemic approach to CSE for social workers in a South London borough, practitioners had reported feeling under-confident and lacking in knowledge in relation to CSE and hindered by prescriptive assessment protocols that were too generalist and non-systemic (Barlow, 2017). In 2016, Haughey heard from police investigators who were struggling to properly evidence 'exploitation'.

Fieldwork in the UK that has informed this book found that there is very little assistance available to safeguarding investigators (social workers) within the Children Act 1989 and Working Together 2015 (and now 2018, and any of its supplementary guidance) nor the Community Care Act 2014 and its provisions for safeguarding vulnerable adults. Many considered that the introduction of the Modern Slavery Act 2015 was to some extent prompting new lines of enquiry, offering statutory mechanisms that had the potential to help them in the context of extra-familial exploitation and abuse. Many professionals have also recognised that victims of trafficking and modern slavery are highly vulnerable to secondary victimisation through criminal justice and social care systems (by being considered perpetrators of petty crime rather than being identified as victims of exploitation) and were frequently frustrated in finding opportunities to safeguard some victims while simultaneously avoiding criminalising them (Murphy et al, 2022). The sad irony is that often, criminalising some victims, especially victims of criminal exploitation, seems to be first point at which services and resources are available to assist them or extricate them from the exploitation.

The Council of Europe Trafficking Convention incorporates non-prosecution principles, but rapid identification is crucial to avoiding the prosecution of victims of trafficking, especially children, because of their vulnerability to re-trafficking and further exploitation. However, the existing system is often unable to achieve this rapidly enough. National Referral Mechanism (NRM) processes for decision-making and communication can be a serious constraint upon safeguarding trafficked and vulnerable people. Some professionals in focus groups, seminars and conferences at which the Circles of Analysis model has been presented considered that the NRM decision delays in the UK were also evidence of a conflict between government policies on human trafficking and immigration – a view that has been recently echoed by Kidd, Falkner, and Arocha (2019).

There is a tendency among many prosecutors and defence lawyers to confuse the defence relating to coercive control with the 'duress' principle. The two principles are quite different from each other and deal with different circumstances, but confusion exists throughout the criminal justice and social care systems, which become muddled with questions of consent and rational choice ('lifestyle choices'). There remains a lack of awareness of the nature and processes of exploitation, the relationships between those that are being exploited and their exploiters, and the factors that contribute to and maintain the opportunity to multiply exploit a person.

The problems identified by my research, and in the wider literature cited in this book, indicate that safeguarding systems not only fail to keep up with the evolution of human trafficking, modern slavery and other forms of exploitation, but even contribute to its maintenance and development: they fail to anticipate and adapt, always attempting to bolt on new procedures and standards to safeguarding and law enforcement practice which ultimately are overly simplistic, reductive definitions of the problem and result in the development of increasingly reactive and self-defeating flow-chart interventions that lack any theoretical footing.

Language and flawed logic

Our discursive use of 'exploitation', 'trafficking' and 'modern slavery' denotes certain types of criminal activity and these are rather technical terms with definitions of specific offences and relevant 'points to prove'. While the terminology offers points of reference against which decisions about statutory interventions such as safeguarding measures, investigation and prosecution can be formulated, they do not adequately describe the phenomenon itself and so do not actually help practitioners understand what they are dealing with or even looking for (Barlow, 2019, 2022; Heys et al, 2022). Such terminology is therefore not helpful in developing prevention strategies, since, in systemic terms, they refer only to an output of a system, not the mechanisms by which the system operates. The limited ability of professional practitioners to identify and respond to cases of human trafficking, modern slavery and exploitation is in no small part symptomatic of fundamentally flawed policies and procedures to which they are tied.

Understanding of such cases is not facilitated by labels, nor is it gained by identifying any similarities that they have and formulating typologies or 'profiles': the cases are too complex and multifactorial. If a pattern of behaviour does not score highly on a checklist or does not fit the typology's descriptive definition of trafficking or modern slavery, it is considered not present or is interpreted as a different type of problem, and this contributes to siloing of decision-making, organisational structures and interventions. The problem of siloing and human trafficking, modern slavery or other forms of exploitation is symptomatic of efforts to label phenomena. The reality is that survivors' experiences of, and involvement in, exploitative practices varies in terms of the aetiology of their involvement and relationships with other potentially suitable targets and with the perpetrators of their exploitation, and their interactions with the environments from which they and the perpetrators emerge. This may be a reason why a stand-alone definition of trafficking and modern slavery is so difficult to formulate.

Limitations

The research that informs this book has benefitted greatly from the enthusiastic willingness of academics and practitioners to engage both through informal interviews, colloquia and the formal focus groups. The fact that the participants were all practitioners that shared an interest in the topic (which motivated them to take part) may justify criticism that the model received affirmation from like-minded professionals and too few cynics. This points to certain assumptions in the research itself: it has taken for granted that CCE exists and that the pattern of behaviour that is identified and defined as CCE within this research is exploitative. The working definition of CCE used within this thesis has not been challenged or criticised. This may in part be due to the nature of the sample group: the professionals that were recruited for participation in the focus groups all held statutory decision-making responsibilities. The fieldwork for this research has not therefore incorporated any contributions from non-statutory agencies or actors. This was a deliberate decision in the planning of the research method and is acknowledged as a self-imposed limitation.

A second limitation is the absence of direct involvement of children that have been trafficked and criminally exploited or the perpetrators. A children's rights perspective is adopted within the body of the thesis (see, for instance, Chapters 2 and 3) and constructs of childhood and who is a child (Ballet et al, 2002; Munroe, 2002; Shannahan, 2007) are discussed. There are always serious ethical concerns that arise given the inherent vulnerability of child participants, particularly with children that have endured traumatic experiences. The decision was made to use secondary open sources as illustrative case studies as a non-intrusive solution to the problem of including the child's voice though a survivor's valuation of the model would be of considerable interest.

Similarly, there were significant ethical issues in identifying and recruiting perpetrators of CCE in enough numbers and diversity to reflect the complexity and diversity of the phenomenon. Consequently, to do so was beyond the scope of this thesis. As with the child's voice, secondary sources (including news interviews such as Paco in Chapter 2 and recent research by Broad assessing convicted traffickers of human beings) have been included. Nevertheless, the absence of contributions from both children and perpetrators is acknowledged as a further self-imposed limitation of this research.

Weaknesses in policy and statutory guidance have been identified in this thesis through the review of official reports, guidance documents and the professional and academic literature. The identification of these weaknesses has been supported by the professionals that have participated in the focus groups and in other informal interviews and discussions. The voice of the policy makers is not included and so there has been no opportunity for rebuttal or acknowledgement of the criticisms that have been raised.

Future directions and further research

The current responses to human trafficking and modern slavery are inconsistent and inefficient. The overarching policies of both local and national, and international authorities are reactive and fail to guide or support those that are charged with the responsibility of identifying and investigating the perpetrators of criminal exploitation and safeguarding the people that are targeted for exploitation. Our systems are therefore currently, and perhaps ironically, a part of the conducive environment. The Circles of Analysis model provides a framework for local and national strategic needs analysis and for the development of policies and procedures that understand that (a) children who are suitable targets for exploitation exist relationally to their abusers and their environments, and (b) that the exploitation is an output of a complex of systems with multiple possibility spaces in which to intervene.

Further development of theory

The Circles of Analysis model provides a starting point for practitioners to evaluate the facts of the case, organise their evidence and plan their assessment, investigations, interventions and advice to colleagues and other agencies. Similarly, the model provides a framework for further development of knowledge about exploitative relationships, patterns of coercive and controlling behaviour, resilience and vulnerability.

This book has taken the opportunity to apply criminological theory to the wider problem of human trafficking, slavery, exploitation and abuse, and found that criminological knowledge of violence, victimology, organised crime and criminal justice processes is a positive contribution to the field of safeguarding of children and vulnerable adults. The Circles of Analysis model is a theoretical framework that will contribute to further research and development in this field but the model itself will also be further refined through such critical application.

The model provides a framework for further research and a framework for understanding organised crime both in terms of structures and activities and also development over time. Just as the model assists in identifying and analysing complex abuses and exploitation of children and vulnerable adults, it has the potential to inform strategic and tactical responses to organised crime, as well as providing a theoretical framework for research of organised crime, organised crime groups and networks.

Development of professional practice

Case analysis using the Circles of Analysis model as a theoretical framework can enable police and prosecutors to develop victimless prosecutions and relieve the burden upon victims to make a disclosure before they are emotionally, psychologically and physically safe enough to do so (Bristow, 2019).

The model has been supported by professionals as a robust theory for various forms of exploitation and processes of human trafficking. Furthermore, they advised against turning the model into a manual. The clarity of the graphic representation was considered by them to be extremely accessible and practical in assisting practitioners (at all levels and across agencies) to organise their evidence and make their enquiries. For non-specialist practitioners, however, something that provides greater guidance but allows for professional discretion in judgement and decision-making is likely to be appropriate. The model, therefore, offers the foundation for the development of structured professional judgement (SPJ) protocols such as the Adapted SIPPS tool for CSE (Barlow, 2017), the HCR-20 Violence Risk Assessment Protocol (Douglas et al, 2013) and the Stalking Assessment and Management Guidelines (Kropp, Hart, and Lyon, 2008). As a theory, however, it needs to be primarily disseminated through professional training and continuing professional development, and tested in different contexts and jurisdictions. This is important to maintain the relevance and utility of the model and to ensure it is able to evolve as patterns of trafficking and modern slavery also evolve.

While it has been suggested that the model may be transferable to areas such as general child abuse, domestic abuse, gangs and radicalisation or counterterrorism, this possibility needs to be studied further, and the model may require development and adaptation to the specifics of those problems.

Final comment

The Circles of Analysis model represents a synthesis of extant theory for the purpose of generating a new theory of human trafficking and modern slavery. As it has developed, so have new opportunities for enquiry and acquisition of knowledge in this complex and challenging field. The current iteration of the model presented in this book is co-created by me as the researcher and the experts that have contributed their insights and frontline experience. It is they who have already found ways to apply and develop my original model. I hope that this collaboration, these multi-disciplinary contributions, mean that this theory has a life beyond academia and will be relevant, now and in the future, to the worldwide challenge of trafficking and modern slavery. Consequently, this theory will necessarily be an ongoing work and this thesis merely a first step in a new direction.

References

Alach, Z.J. (2011) 'An incipient taxonomy of organised crime', *Trends in Organised Crime*, 14(1): 56–72.

Allain, J. (2010) '*Rantsev v Cyprus and Russia*: the European Court of Human Rights and trafficking as slavery', *Human Rights Law Review*, 10(3): 246–557.

Amnesty International (2004) *Lives Blown Apart: Crimes Against Women in Times of Conflict – Stop Violence Against Women*, Amnesty International, International Secretariat.

Anti-Slavery International (2010) 'London's MET Police help bust child trafficking gang in Romania'. Retrieved 27 October 2016 from www.antislavery.org/latest/londons-met-police-help-bust-child-trafficking-gang-romania/#:~:text=A%20gang%20of%20Romanian%20child,supported%20by%20London's%20Met%20police

Anti-Slavery International (2014) *Trafficking for Forced Criminal Activities and Begging in Europe: Exploratory Study and Good Practice Examples*, London: Anti-Slavery International.

Aziani, A., Bertoni, G.A., Jofre, M., and Riccardi, M. (2023) 'COVID-19 and organized crime: strategies employed by criminal groups to increase their profits and power in the first months of the pandemic', *Trends in Organized Crime*, 26(2): 114–35.

Baker, N.D. and Leão, G. (2021) 'Parties of crime? Brazil's facções criminosa's: good governance and bad government', *Small Wars Journal*, 19.

Bales, K. (2012) *Disposable People: New Slavery in the Global Economy* (revised edn), Berkeley, CA: University of California Press.

Ballet, J., Bukuth, A., Rakotonirinhanahary, F., Rakotonirinhanhary, M., Divinagracia, E., and Detreuilh, C. (2002) 'Family rationales behind child begging in Antananarivo', *Population* (English edn), 65(4): 695–712.

Barlow, C. (2017) 'The Adapted SIPPS for CSE: evaluation of a pilot project in a South London borough', *European Review of Organised Crime*, 4(2): 101–27.

Barlow, C. (2019) *Child Criminal Exploitation: A New Systemic Model to Improve Professional Assessment, Investigation and Intervention*, Hull: University of Hull.

Barlow, C. (2022) 'Victims perpetrating a crime: a critique of responses to forced criminality and modern slavery in the UK Courts', in C. Murphy, R. Lazzarino, and Hodges (eds) *Modern Slavery and Human Trafficking: The Victim Journey*, London: Policy Press.

Barlow, C. (2023) 'British victims of modern slavery: journeys into criminal exploitation and alternative interventions', *2022 Conference: Reimagining Criminological Futures: New Criminologies in a Changing World*, Letchworth Garden City: British Society of Criminology, pp 51–8. Retrieved 29 June 2024 from www.britsoccrim.org/wp-content/uploads/2022/12/BSC-Online-Journal-2022.pdf

Barlow, C. and Murphy, C. (forthcoming) *The Organisation of Modern Slavery*.

Barlow, C., Green, S., Kidd, A., and Darby, B. (2021) 'Circles of Analysis: a systemic model of child criminal exploitation', *Journal of Children's Services*, 17(3): 157–74.

Barlow, J., Fisher, J.D., and Jones, D. (2012) *Systematic Review of Models of Analysing Significant Harm*, London: Department for Education.

Bennett, T. and Holloway, K. (2004) 'Gang membership, drugs and crime in the UK', *British Journal of Criminology*, 44(3): 305–23.

Berg, R. and Varsori, A. (2020) 'COVID-19 is increasing the power of Brazil's criminal groups', 28 May, London school of Economics. Retrieved 8 July 2024 from https://blogs.lse.ac.uk/latamcaribbean/2020/05/28/covid-19-is-increasing-the-power-of-brazils-criminal-groups/

Bingham, C. (2010) *Child Poverty Relating to Gypsy and Traveller Children and Young People in Sussex*, Friends, Families and Travellers. Retrieved 8 July 2024 from www.gypsy-traveller.org/wp-content/uploads/2017/03/poverty-needs-assessment-report-youth.pdf

Bjerregaard, B. (2002) 'Self-definitions of gang membership and involvement in delinquent activities', Youth & Society, 34(1): 31–54.

Blum, A. (1996) 'Panic and fear: on the phenomenology of desperation', Sociological Quarterly, 37(4): 673–98.

Blumer, H. (1971) 'Social problems as collective behaviour', Social Problems, 18(3): 298–306.

Bourdieu, P. (1986) 'The form of capital', in J. Richardson (ed) Handbook of Theory and Research for the Sociology of Education, New York: Greenwood, pp 241–58.

Bristow, J. (2019) A Police Perspective on Modern Slavery and Human Trafficking, London: National Crime Agency.

Broad, R. (2018) 'Assessing convicted traffickers: negotiating migration, employment and opportunity through restricted networks', Howard Journal of Crime and Justice, 57(1): 37–56.

Broad, R. and Turnbull, N. (2018) 'From human trafficking to modern slavery: the development of anti-trafficking policy in the UK', European Journal on Criminal Policy and Research, 25: 119–33.

Brotherton, V. and Waters, F. (2013) Victim or Criminal? Trafficking for Forced Criminal Exploitation in Europe: UK Chapter, ECPAT. Retrieved 3 November 2016 from www.antislavery.org/wp-content/uploads/2017/01/Criminal-or-victim-UK.pdf

Byrne, D. and Callaghan, G. (2014) Complexity Theory and the Social Sciences: The State of the Art, London and New York: Routledge.

Calouri, J., Hutt, O., Olajole, P., and Kirk, E. (2022) Fixing Neverland: Social Media and Serious Youth Violence, London: Crest Advisory.

Cantor, C. and Price, J. (2007) 'Traumatic entrapment, appeasement and complex post-traumatic stress disorder: evolutionary perspectives of hostage reactions, domestic abuse and the Stockholm Syndrome', Australian & New Zealand Journal of Psychiatry, 41(5): 377–84.

CEOP and The British Embassy, Hanoi (2011) The Trafficking of Women and Children from Vietnam, Hanoi: CEOP.

Cheng, S. (2017) 'A critical engagement with the "pull and push" model: human trafficking and migration into sex work', in R. Piotrowicz, C. Rijken, and B. Uhl (eds) Routledge Handbook of Human Trafficking, London and New York: Routledge, pp 499–510.

Christie, N. (1986) 'The ideal victim', in E.A. Fattah (ed) *From Crime Policy to Victim Policy*, London: Palgrave Macmillan, pp 17–30.

Chuang, J.A. (2014) 'Exploitation creep and the unmaking of human trafficking law', *American Journal of International Law*, 108(4): 609–49.

Clement, V., Rigaud, K.K., de Sherbinin, A., Jones, B., Adamo, S., Schewe, J. et al (2021) *Groundswell Part 2: Acting on Internal Climate Migration*, Washington, DC: World Bank.

Connelly, B.L., Certo, S.T., Ireland, D., and Reutzel, C.R. (2011) 'Signaling theory: a review and assessment', *Journal of Management*, 37(1): 39–67.

Coomans, F., Grünfeld, F., and Kamminga, M.T. (2010) 'Methods of human rights research: a primer', *Human Rights Quarterly*, 32(1): 179–86.

Cooper, C., Hesketh, O., Ellis, N., and Fair, A. (2017) *A Typology of Modern Slavery Offences in the UK, Research Report 93*, London: Home Office.

Cooray, D.M. (2017) 'Globalisation and its effects on human trafficking: a legal perspective from Asia'. Retrieved 8 July 2024 from www.researchgate.net/publication/309608905_Globalization_and_its_Effects_on_Human_Trafficking_A_Legal_Perspective_from_Asia/link/5bc3376b92851c88fd6a09eb/download

Cottrell-Boyce, J. (2013) 'Ending gang and youth violence: a critique', *Youth Justice*, 13(3): 193–206.

Council of Europe (2005) Official Texts. European Court of Human Rights. Retrieved 8 July 2024 from www.echr.coe.int/pages/home.aspx?p=basictexts

Clarke, R.V. and Cornish, D.B. (1985) 'Modeling offenders' decisions: a framework for research and policy', in M. Tonry and N. Morris (eds), *Crime and Justice: An Annual Review of Research, Vol. 6*, Chicago: University of Chicago Press, pp 147–85.

Cressey, D.R. (1969) *The Theft of the Nation: Structure and Operations of Organised Crime in America*, New York, Evanston and London: Harper and Row.

Davis, D. and Hilgers, T. (2022) 'The pandemic and organized crime in urban Latin America: new sovereignty arrangements or business as usual?' *Journal of Illicit Economies and Development*, 4(3): 241–56.

Decker, S. and Kempf-Leonard, K. (1991) 'Constructing gangs: the social definition of youth activities', *Criminal Justice Policy Review*, 5(4): 271–91.

Densley, J.R. (2012) 'Street gang recruitment signalling, screening, and selection', *Social Problems*, 59(3): 301–21.

Douglas, K.S., Hart, S.D., Webster, C.D., and Belfrage, H. (2013) *The HCR-20v3: Assessing Risk for Violence: User Guide*, Mental Health, Law, and Social Policy Institute, Simon Fraser University.

Duong, W.N. (2001) 'Gender equality and women's issues in Vietnam: the Vietnamese woman-warrior and poet', *Pacific Rim Law and Policy Journal Association*, 10(2): 191–326.

Dwyer, P., Hodkinson, S., Lewis, H., and Waite, L. (2016) 'Socio-legal status and experiences of forced labour among asylum seekers and refugees in the UK', *Journal of International and Comparative Social Policy*, 32(3): 182–98.

ECPAT UK (2010) *ECPAT UK Briefing Paper Child Trafficking – Begging and Organised Crime*, London: ECPAT.

Edwards, A. and Gill, P. (2004) *Transnational Organised Crime: Perspectives on Global Security*, London and New York: Routledge.

Elster, J. (2001) 'Rational Choice theory: cultural concerns', *International Encyclopedia of the Social and Behavioural Sciences*, 21(1): 5–33.

European Commission (2022) *Report on the Progress Made in the Fight Against Trafficking in Human Beings (Fourth Report)*, Brussels: European Commission.

European Court of Human Rights (2014) *Guide on Article 4 of the Convention – Prohibition of Slavery and Forced Labour*, Council of Europe/European Court of Human Rights.

European Roma Rights Centre and People In Need (2011) *Breaking the Silence: Trafficking in Romani Communities*, European Roma Rights Centre and People In Need.

Europol (2019) 'Operation GOLF'. Retrieved 8 July 2024 from www.europol.europa.eu/activities-services/europol-in-action/operations/operation-golf

Europol (2022) *Early Warning Notive: War in Ukraine – Refugees Arriving to the EU From Ukraine at Risk of Exploitation as Part of THB*, The Hague: Europol Operations Directorate.

Fatić, A. (1999) 'Organised crime in Eastern Europe', *SEER: Journal for Labor and Social Affairs in Eastern Europe*, 2(1): 77–85.

Felitti, V.J., Anda, R.F., Nordenberg, D., Williamson, D.F., Spitz, A.M., Edwards, V., et al (1998) 'Relationship of childhood abuse and household dysfunction to many of the leading causes of death in adults: the Adverse Childhood Experiences (ACE) study', *American Journal of Preventive Medicine*, 14(4): 245–58.

Felson, M. and Cohen, L.E. (1980) 'Human ecology and crime: a routine activity approach', *Human Ecology*, 8(4): 389–406.

Field, F., Butler-Sloss, E., and Miller, M. (2019) *Final Report of the Independent Review of the Modern Slavery Act 2015*, London: Home Office.

Finckenauer, J.O. (2005) 'Problems of definition: what is organized crime?' *Trends in Organized Crime*, 8: 63–83.

Finkelhor, D. (2008) *Childhood Victimisation: Violence, Crime and Abuse in the Lives of Young People*, New York: Oxford University Press.

Firmin, C. (2017) *Contextual Safeguarding*, Bedford: University of Bedfordshire/Contextual Safeguarding Network.

Firmin, C., Curtis, G., Fritz, D., Olaitan, P., Latchford, L., Lloyd, J., et al (2016) *Towards a Contextual Response to Peer-on-Peer Abuse: Research and Resources from MsUnderstood Local Site Work 2013–2016*, Luton: University of Bedfordshire.

Fitch, K. (2009) *Teenagers at Risk: Safeguarding Needs of Young People in Gangs and Violent Peer Groups*, NSPCC.

Freedom, R. and des Avocats Internationaux, B. (2011) 'Restavèk: the persistence of child labor and slavery', Twelfth Session of the Working Group on the UPR, Human Rights Council.

Frontex (2021) *Frontex Risk Analysis for 2022–2023*, Warsaw: Frontex.

Fuchs, C. (2018) 'Authoritarian capitalism, authoritarian movements and authoritarian communication', *Media, Culture & Society*, 40(5): 779–91.

Fudge, J. (2018) 'Modern slavery, unfree labour and the labour market: the social dynamics of legal characterization', *Social and Legal Studies*, 27(4): 414–34.

Fuller, R.C. and Myers, R.R. (1941) 'The natural history of a social problem', *American Sociological Review*, 6(3): 320–9.

Gadd, D. and Broad, R. (2018) 'Troubling recognitions in British responses to modern slavery', *British Journal of Criminology*, 58(6): 1440–61.

Gear, C., Eppel, E., and Koziol-Mclain, J. (2018) 'Advancing Complexity theory as a qualitative research methodology', *International Journal of Qualitative Methods*, 17(1): 1–10.

Gelfland, M.J., Raver, J.L., Nishii, L., and Leslie, L. (2011) 'Differences between tight and loose cultures: a 33-nation study', *Science*, 332(6003): 1100–4.

Giambetta, D. (2009) *Codes of the Underworld: How Criminals Communicate*, Princeton, NJ: Princeton University Press.

Green, S.T., Heys, A., and Barlow, C. (forthcoming) 'The conducive environment: reconceptualising the exploitation of human beings'.

Griffith, J.L., Griffith, M.E., and Slovik, L.S. (1990) 'Mind–body problems in family therapy: contrasting first- and second-order cybernetics approaches', *Family Process*, 29(1): 13–28.

Gross, A. and Thomas, C. (2017) 'The new abolitionism, international law, and the memory of slavery', *Law and History Review*, 35(1): 99–118.

Gurung, A. and Clark, A.D. (2018) 'The perfect storm: the impact of disaster severity on internal human trafficking', *International Area Studies Review*, 21(4): 302–22.

Hannan, C.E. and Hackathorn, J. (2022) 'Desperate times call for a desperate measure: validating a measure of state desperation', *Current Psychology*, 41: 4490–500.

Harding, S. (2020) *County Lines*, Bristol: Bristol University Press.

Hart, S.D., Kropp, R., and Laws, D.R. (2003) *The Risk for Sexual Violence Protocol (RSVP)*, Mental Health, Law and Policy Institute, Simon Fraser University.

Hart, S.D., Kropp, R.P., Laws, R.D., Klaver, J., Logan, C., and Watt, K.A. (2003) *The Risk For Sexual Violence Protocol (RSVP): Structured Professional Guidelines for Assessing Risk of Sexual Violence*, British Columbia, Canada.

Hassett, P. and Stevens, I. (2014) 'Child protection and complexity', in A. Pycroft and C. Bortollas (eds) *Applying Complexity Theory*, Bristol: Policy Press.

Haughey, C. (2016a) Personal Contact.

Haughey, C. (2016b) *The Modern Slavery Act Review: One Year On*, London: Home Office.

Henkoma, S. (2022) Alex's story: a case of child criminal exploitation (C. Barlow, Interviewer).

Henry-Lee, A. (2005) 'Convergence? The Lewis model and the rights-based approach to development', *Social and Economic Studies*, 54(4, Special Issue on Sir Arthur Lewis, Part II): 91–121.

Heys, A. (2023) *From Conflict to Modern Slavery: The Drivers and Deterrents*, Oxford: Oxford University Press.

Heys, A., Barlow, C., Murphy, C., and McKee, A. (2022) 'A review of modern slavery in Britain: understanding the unique experience of British victims, and why it matters', *Journal of Victimology and Victim Justice*, 5(1): 54–70.

Hirsch, A. (2015) 'Children "Trafficked" Around UK by Drug Dealers'. Retrieved 8 July 2024 from http://news.sky.com/story/children-trafficked-around-uk-by-drug-dealers-10375380

HM Government (2014) *Modern Slavery Strategy*, London: Stationery Office.

HM Government (2015) *Working Together to Safeguard Children: A Guide to Inter-Agency Working to Safeguard and Promote Welfare of Children*, London: HM Government.

HM Government (2017) *Criminal Exploitation of Children and Vulnerable Adults: County Lines*, London: Home Office.

Hodgson, G.M. (2012) 'On the limits of Rational Choice theory', *Economic Thought*, 1: 94–108.

Hoshi, B. (2013) 'The trafficking defence: a proposed model for the non-criminalisation of trafficked persons in international law', *Groningen Journal of International Law*, 1(2).

House of Commons Home Affairs Committee (2023) Oral evidence: Human Trafficking, HC 1142, London: House of Commons.

International Labour Organization (1930) ILO Forced Labour Convention, 1930 (No. 29). Retrieved 8 July 2024 from www.ilo.org/wcmsp5/groups/public/---asia/---ro-bangkok/documents/genericdocument/wcms_346435.pdf

International Labour Organization (2009) *Operational Indicators of Trafficking in Human Beings*. Retrieved 8 July 2024 from www.ilo. org/sites/default/files/wcmsp5/groups/public/@ed_norm/ @declaration/documents/publication/wcms_105023.pdf

Ionescu, I. and Fusu-Plaiasu, G. (2008) *FRA Thematic Study on Child Trafficking Romania*. European Union Agency for Fundamental Rights (FRA). European Commission.

Janak, T.C. (2000) 'Haiti's "Restavec" slave children: difficult choices, difficult lives ... yet ... Lespwa fe Viv', *International Journal of Children's Rights*, 8, 321–31.

Jay, A. (2014) *Independent Inquiry into Child Sexual Exploitation in Rotherham 1997–2013*, Rotherham Metropolitan Borough Council.

Jennings, P. (2014) 'Risk, attractors and organisational behaviour: whole systems approaches to criminal justice and social work', in A. Pycroft and C. Bortollas (eds) *Applying Complexity Theory*, Bristol: Policy Press.

Jesperson, S. and Henriksen, R. (2023) 'Criminal Pyramid scheme: organised crime recruitment strategies', in C. Murphy and R. Lazzarino (eds) *Modern Slavery and Human Trafficking: The Victim Journey*, Bristol: Policy Press, pp 25–40.

Jovanovic, M. (2017) 'The principle of non-punishment', *Journal of Trafficking and Human Exploitation*, 1(1): 41–76.

Kalmar, D.A. and Sternberg, R.J. (1988) 'Theory knitting: an integrative approach to theory development', *Philosophical Psychology*, 1(2): 153–70.

Kara, S. (2011) 'Designing more effective laws against human trafficking', *Northwestern Journal of International Human Rights*, 9(2): 124–47.

Kelly, E. (2002) *Journeys of Jeopardy: A Review of Research on Trafficking in Women and Children in Europe*, United Nations. Retrieved 8 July 2024 from https://publications.iom.int/sys tem/files/pdf/mrs_11_2002.pdf

Kelly, L. (2007) 'A conducive context: trafficking of persons in Central Asia', in M. Lee (ed) *Human Trafficking*, London and New York: Routledge, pp 73–91.

Kidd, A., Faulkner, E., and Arocha, L. (2019) 'How UK asylum system creates perfect conditions for modern slavery and exploitation to thrive'. Retrieved 8 July 2024 from https://theconversation.com//how-uk-asylum system-creates-perfect-conditions-for modern slavery-and exploitation-to-thrive-113778

Knowsley Council (2015) *Child Exploitation: JSNA Report*, Knowsley Council.

Kropp, R.P., Hart, S.D., and Lyon, D.R. (2008) *Guidelines for Stalking Assessment and Management (SAM) User Manual*, ProActive ReSolutions.

Landman, T. (2018) 'Out of the shadows: trans-disciplinary research on modern slavery', *Peace Human Rights Governance*, 2(2): 143–62.

Levi, M. (1998) 'Perspectives on "organised crime": an overview', *The Howards Journal*, 37(4): 335–45.

Lewis, H., Dwyer, P., Hodkinson, S., and Waite, L. (2014) *Precarious Lives: Forced Labour, Exploitation and Asylum*, Bristol: Policy Press.

Longfield, A. (2019) *Keeping Kids Safe: Improving Safeguarding Responses to Gang Violence and Criminal Exploitation*. London: Office of the Children's Commissioner for England.

Love, A. (2017) Personal Contact (C. Barlow, Interviewer).

Lynham, S.A. (2002) 'The general method of theory-building research in applied disciplines', *Advances in Developing Human Resources*, 4(3): 221–41.

Lyons, P., Doueck, H.J., and Wodarski, J.S. (1996) 'Risk assessment for child protective services: a review of the empirical literature on instrument performance', *Social Work Research*, 20(3): 143–55.

Malangone, A. (2024) Personal Contact.

Maltz, M.D. (1976) 'On defining "organized crime": the development of a definition and a typology', *Crime and Delinquency*, 22(3): 338–46.

Manson, S.M. (2001) 'Simplifying complexity: a review of Complexity theory', *Geoforum*, 32(3): 405–14.

Maschi, T. (2016) *Applying a Human Rights Approach to Social Work Research and Evaluation: A Rights Research Manifesto* (1st edn), Cham, Heidelberg, New York, Dordrecht and London: Springer.

Maslow, A.H. ([1943] 2014) *A Theory of Human Motivation* (2014 edn), Floyd, VA: Sublime.

Maurer, A. (2012) '"Social Embeddedness" viewed from an institutional perspective, revision of a core principle of new economic sociology with special regard to Max Weber', *Polish Sociological Review*, 180(4): 475–96.

McClintock, M. (n.d.) 'A basic approach to human rights research'. Retrieved 7 December 2018 from http://humanri ghtshistory.umich.edu/research-and-advocacy/basic-approach-to-human-rights-research/

McDermott, F. (2014) 'Complexity theory, trans-disciplinary working and reflective practice', in A. Pycroft and C. Bartollas (eds) *Applying Complexity Theory: Whole Systems Approaches to Criminal Justice and Social Work*, Bristol: Bristol University Press.

McKinney, J.C. (1969) 'Typification, typologies and sociological theory', *Social Forces*, 48(1): 1–12.

McMillan, A. (2022) 'The global assault on rule of law', International Bar Association. Retrieved 8 July 2024 from www.ibanet.org/The-global-assault-on-rule-of-law

Miller, J. (2009) 'Young women and street gangs', in M.A. Zahn (ed) *The Delinquent Girl*, Philadelphia, PA: Temple University Press, pp 207–24.

Moore, M.H. (1995) 'Public health and criminal justice approaches to health', in M. Tonry and D.P. Farrington (eds) *Building a Safer Society: Strategic Approaches to Crime Prevention*, Chicago and London: University of Chicago Press, pp 237–62.

Morgan, D. (2010) 'The growth of medical tourism', *OECD Observer*, 281: 12–13.

Munroe, E. (2002) *Effective Child Protection*, London: Sage.

Murphy, C.A., Heys, A., Barlow, C., and Wilkinson, S. (2022) *Identifying Pathways to Support British Victims of Modern Slavery towards Safety and Recovery: A Scoping Study*, Twickenham: Bakhita Centre, St Mary's University.

Musto, J.L. and Boyd, D. (2014) 'The trafficking–technology nexus', *Social Politics*, 21(3): 461–83.

National Crime Agency (2015) *NCA Strategic Assessment: Nature and Scale of Human Trafficking in 2014*. National Crime Agency.

Nawala, P. (2023) 'International legal framework on human trafficking and criminal liability on traffickers', *Wukari International Studies Journal*, 7(1): 372–86.

Neuborne, B. (2019) *When at Times the Mob Is Swayed: A Citizen's Guide to Defending Our Republic*, New York: The New Press.

Newburn, T. (2012) *Criminology* (2nd edn), London and New York: Routledge.

Nicholls, C.M., Cockbain, E., Brayley, H., Harvey, S., Fox, C., Paskell, C., et al (2014) *Research on the Sexual Exploitation of Boys and Young Men: A UK Scoping Study Summary of Finding*, Barnardo's.

O'Connell Davidson, J. (2010) 'New slavery, old binaries: human trafficking and the borders of "freedom"', *Global Networks*, 10(2): 246–61.

O'Connell Davidson, J. (2015) '"Things" are not what they seem: on persons, things, slaves, and the new abolitionist movement', *Current Legal Problem*, 69(1): 227.

Ofsted (2018) 'Protecting children from criminal exploitation, human trafficking and modern slavery: an addendum', p 4. Retrieved 8 July 2024 from https://assets.publishing.service.gov. uk/media/5bebe2ac40f0b667b363e279/Protecting_children_ from_criminal_exploitation_human_trafficking_modern_ slavery_addendum_141118.pdf

Pawson, R. and Tilley, N. (1997) *Realist Evaluation*, London: Sage.

Pehlić, A. (2020) 'Occurrence of human trafficking in a conflict/peacebuilding context: Bosnian experience', in J. Muraszkiewicz, T. Fenton, and H. Watson (eds) *Human Trafficking in Conflict: Context, Causes and the Military*, Cham: Palgrave Macmillan, pp 123–41.

Perrow, C. (1999) *Normal Accidents: Living with High-Risk Technologies* (updated edn), Princeton, NJ: Princeton University Press.

Picarelli, J.T. (2002) *Trafficking, Slavery, and Peacekeeping: The Need for a Comprehensive Training Program*, conference report hosted by the Transnational Crime and Corruption Centre, American University and the UN Interregional Crime and Justice Research Institute, pp 9–10.

Pitts, J. (2007) *Reluctant Gangsters: Youth Gangs in Waltham Forest*. Retrieved 8 July 2024 from www.wfcw.org/docs/reluctant-gangsters.pdf

Potrafke, N. (2015) 'The evidence on globalisation', *World Economy*, 38(3): 509–52.

Pycroft, A. and Bartollas, C. (2014) *Applying Complexity Theory: Whole System Approaches to Criminal Justice and Social Work*, Bristol: Policy Press.

Quirke, J. (2006) 'The anti-slavery project: linking the historical and contemporary', *Human Rights Quarterly*, 28(3): 565–98.

Raman, V. (2000) 'Politics of childhood: perspectives from the south', *Economic and Political Weekly*, 35(48): 4055–64.

Ravnbøl, C.I. (2019) 'Patchwork economies in Europe: economic strategies among homeless Romanian Roma in Copenhagen', in T. Magazzini and S. Piemontese (eds) *Constructing Roma Migrants*, London: Springer, pp 209–26.

Robinson, G., McLean, R., and Densley, J. (2018) 'Working county lines: child criminal exploitation and illicit drug dealing in Glasgow and Merseyside', *International Journal of Therapy and Comparative Criminology*, 63(5): 694–711.

Rosenzweig-Ziff, D., Stanley-Becker, I., and Glucroft, W.N. (2022) 'With mostly women and children fleeing Ukraine, European authorities fear a surge in human trafficking', 17 March, *Washington Post*. Retrieved 8 July 2024 from www.washingtonpost.com/world/2022/03/17/human-trafficking-refugees-ukraine-war/

Rudd, A. (2017) 'Inaugural International Conference of the Centre for the Study of Modern Slavery', Twickenham: Centre for the Study of Modern Slavery.

Samarasinghe, V. (2003) 'Confronting globalization in anti-trafficking strategies in Asia', *Brown Journal of World Affairs*, 10(1): 91–104.

Scheptycki, J. (2003) 'The governance of organised crime', *Canadian Journal of Sociology/Cahiers Canadiens de Sociologie*, 28(4): 489–516.

Schneider, J. and Schneider, P. (2008) 'The anthropology of crime and criminalisation', *Annual Review of Anthropology*, 37: 351–73.

Schuler, S.R., Anh, H.T., Ha, V., Minh, T., Thi, B., and vu Thien, P. (2006) 'Constructions of gender in Vietnam: in pursuit of the "three criteria"', *Culture, Health and Sexuality*, 8(5): 383–94.

Schwartz, K. and Allain, J. (2020) *Antislavery in Domestic Legislation: An Empirical Analysis of National Prohibition Globally*, Nottingham: University of Nottingham.

Sellin, T. (1963) 'Organised crime: a business enterprise', *The Annals of the American Academy*, 347(1): 12–19.

Sergi, A. (2017) *From Mafia to Organised Crime: A Comparative Analysis of Policing Models (Critical Criminological Perspectives)*, London: Palgrave Macmillan.

Setter, C. and Baker, C. (2018) *Child Trafficking in the UK in 2018: A Snapshot*, ECPAT UK.

Shannahan, S. (2007) 'Annual review of sociology', *Annual Reviews*, 407–28.

Shelley, L. (2010) *Human Trafficking: A Global Perspective*, Cambridge: Cambridge University Press.

Shipton, A., Setter, C., and Holmes, L. (2016) *Heading Back to Harm: A Study of Trafficked and Unaccompanied Children Going Missing from Care in the UK*, ECPAT.

Silverstone, D. and Brickell, C. (2017) *Combating Modern Slavery*, London: Anti-Slavery Commissioner's Office.

Smith, C.A. and Miller-De La Cuesta, B. (2011) 'Human trafficking in conflict zones: the role of peacekeepers in the formation of networks', *Human Rights Review*, 12, 287–99.

Southwell, P. (2018) Lawyer (C. Barlow, Interviewer).

Stafford, A., Vincent, S., Parton, N., and Smith, C. (2011) *Child Protection Systems in the United Kingdom: A Comparative Analysis*, London: Jessica Kingsley Publishers.

Stevens, I. and Hassett, P. (2007) 'Applying Complexity theory to risk', *Childhood*, 14(1): 128–44.

Stevenson, L. (2015) 'Social workers to face five years in prison for failing to protect children from sexual abuse, warns Cameron'. Retrieved 20 August 2017 from www.communitycare.co.uk/2015/03/03/social-workers-face-five-years-prison-failing-protect-children-sexual-abuse-warns-cameron/

Stoyanova, V. (2012) 'Dancing on the borders of Article 4: human trafficking and the European Court of Human Rights in the *Rantsev* case', *Netherlands Quarterly of Human Rights*, 30(2): 163–94.

Surtees, R. (2005) *Other Forms of Trafficking in Minors: Articulating Victim Profiles and Conceptualizing Interventions*. NEXUS Institute to Combat Human Trafficking and International Organization for Migration (IOM).

Sykes, G.M. and Matza, D. (2013) 'Techniques of neutralisation', in E. McLaughlin and J. Muncie (eds) *Criminological Perspectives* (3rd edn) Washington, DC: Sage, pp 247–55.

Tihelková, A. (2015) 'Framing the "scroungers": the re-emergence of the stereotype of the undeserving poor and its reflection in the British press', *Brno studies in English*, 41(2): 121–39.

Tyldum, G. and Brunovskis, A. (2005) 'Describing the unobserved: methodological challenges in empirical studies on human trafficking', in F. Laczko and E. Gozdziac (eds) *Data and Research on Human Trafficking: A Global Survey*, International Organization for Migration.

UK Serious Organised Crime (SOC) Strategic Analysis Team (2014) *Intelligence Notification 16 Child Trafficking for Exploitation in Forced Criminal Activities and Forced Begging*, NCIA.

United Nations (1956) 'Supplementary Convention on the Abolition of Slavery, the Slave Trade, and Institutions and Practices Similar to Slavery', New York. Retrieved 30 May 2017 from www.ohchr.org/EN/ProfessionalInterest/Pages/SupplementaryConventionAbolitionOfSlavery.aspx

United Nations (2000) Palermo Protocol. *Protocol to Protect, Suppress and Punish Trafficking in Persons, Especially Women and Children, Supplementing the United Nations Convention Against Transnational Organised Crime*, 2. Palermo: United Nations Office on Drugs and Crime. Retrieved 30 May 2017 from www.unodc.org/documents/treaties/UNTOC/Publications/TOC%20Convention/TOCebook-e.pdf

United Nations (n.d.) Slavery Convention, signed at Geneva on 25 September 1926 and amended by the Protocol. Retrieved 30 May 2017 from www.ohchr.org/EN/ProfessionalInterest/Pages/SlaveryConvention.aspx

United Nations Office on Drugs and Crime (n.d.) *Human Trafficking Indicators.* Retrieved 28 December 2023 from www.unodc.org/pdf/HT_indicators_E_LOWRES.pdf

UN Office of the High Commissioner for Human Rights (OHCHR) (1991) 'Fact Sheet No. 14, Contemporary Forms of Slavery'. Retrieved 30 May 2017 from www.refworld.org/docid/4794773b0.html

US Department of State (2022) *2022 Trafficking in Persons Report: Ukraine*. Retrieved 8 July 2024 from www.state.gov/reports/2022-trafficking-in-persons-report/ukraine/#content

Vandenberg, M. (2018) 'Peacekeeping, human trafficking, and sexual abuse and exploitation', in F. Ní Aoláin, N. Cahn, D.F. Haynes, and N. Valji (eds) *The Oxford Handbook of Gender and Conflict*, Oxford: Oxford University Press.

van der Watt, M. and van der Westhuizen, A. (2017) '(Re)configuring the criminal justice response to human trafficking: a complex systems perspective', *Police Practice and Research*, 18(3): 218–29.

von Lampe, K. (2019) 'Definitions of organised crime'. Retrieved 8 July 2024 from www.organized-crime.de/organizedcrimedefi nitions.htm

Ward, T. and Seigert, R.J. (2002) 'Toward a comprehensive theory of child sexual abuse: a theory knitting perspective', *Psychology, Crime and Law*, 4: 319–51.

Warren, K., Franklin, C., and Streeter, C.L. (1998) 'New directions in systems theory: chaos and complexity', *Social Work*, 43(4): 357–72.

Webster, S., Davidson, J., Bifulco, A., Gottschalk, P., Caretti, V., Pham, T., et al (2012) *European Online Grooming Project: Final Report*, European Union.

Whitaker, A.J., Cheston, L., Tyrell, T., Higgins, M.M., Felix-Baptiste, C., and Harvard, T. (2018) *From Postcodes to Profit: How Gangs Have Changed in Waltham Forest*, London: London South Bank University.

Wood, J. (2019) 'Confronting gang membership and youth violence: intervention challenges', *Criminal Behaviour and Mental Health*, 29(2): 69–73.

Woodiwiss, M. (2004) 'Transnational organised crime: the global reach of an American concept', in A. Edwards and P. Gill (eds) *Transnational Organised Crime: Perspectives on Security*, London and New York: Routledge.

Woodward, A. (2019) 'Climate change: disruption, risk and opportunity', *Global Transitions*, 1: 44–9.

Wulczyn, F., Daro, D., Fluke, J., Feldman, S., Glodek, C., and Lifanda, K. (2010) *Adapting a Systems Approach to Child Protection: Key Concepts and Considerations*, New York: United Nations Children's Fund (UNICEF).

Zahir, H., Southwell, P., Brewer, P., and Harvey, S. (2020) 'Trafficking operatioins and modus operandi', in P. Southwell, M. Brewer, and B. Douglas Jones QC (eds), *Human Trafficking and Modern Slavery Law and Practice*, London: Bloomsbury Professional, pp 533–62.

Zimmerman, C., Hossain, M., Yum, K., Roche, B., Morison, L., and Watts, C. (2006) *Stolen Smiles: The Physical and Psychological Health Consequences of Women and Adolescents Trafficked in Europe*, London: London School of Hygiene and Tropical Medicine.

Index

References to figures appear in *italic* type; those in **bold** type refer to tables. References to footnotes show both the page number and the note number (27n1).

and survival needs 47, 49,
  67, 69, 107
typologies of 15, 16, 45, 92, 175
vulnerability of families to 67–9
and work/labour 47–9
see also child criminal exploitation
  (CCE); human trafficking

F

Fair, A. 108
family(ies)
  -based exploitation 63, 67, 135–6
  and child labour 47, 49
  members, exploitation by 16, 46,
    48, 58, 75, 102, 144, 152–3
  and safeguarding models 10
  vulnerability to exploitation 67–9
  see also domestic servitude
Fatić, A. 51–2
Faulkner, E. 174
favelas 121
Felitti, V.J. 168
Fell, I. 60
Felson, M. 129, 159
Finckenauer, J.O. 57
Finkelhor, D. 168
Firmin, C. 159
Fisher, J.D. 173
focus groups 18, 163, 172–3, 176
forced labour 28n2, 29–30, **31**, 32, 35
  definition of 28
  Van der Mussele v Belgium
    (1983) **31**, 32–4, 38
Forced Labour Convention
  (1930) 28, 29
forced sex work 149, *151*, 152
'4 Ps' paradigm 15
friend–enemy scheme 126–7
Fuchs, C. 126
Fuller, R.C. 109

G

gangs
  communities affected by 136–7
  drug 134, 144–6
  recruitment in 144–5
  street 8, 133–4, 144
  use of social media 60, 61–2
  violence in 145–6
Gelfland, M.J. 114
gender-based violence 102
Giambetta, D. 139–40
globalisation 60, 126

goals
  of actors in complex systems
    72–3, 74
  congruity, between victims and
    perpetrators 131, 132, 134–5,
    136, 141, 144
  and decision-making 125, 139
  and social bonds 119, 120
Green, Simon 13, 43, 47, 97, 114,
  128, 171
Gross, A. 41
Grünfeld, F. 21, 22

H

Haiti
  child trafficking in 117–18
  restavec system in 117
Hart, S.D. 169, 171
Haughey, Caroline 1, 61, 71,
  81, 173
health and social care system
  responses to human trafficking/
    modern slavery 10, 157
  secondary victimisation of
    victims 173–4
Henkoma, Sosa 136–7, 144–6, 152
Henriksen, R. 82, 84
Hesketh, O. 108
Heys, Alicia 13, 43, 47, 77, 97, 106,
  114, 128, 171
hierarchy of needs (Maslow) 74,
  124, 132
Hodgson, G.M. 125, 137–8
Home Office 15, 16, 45, 60
Hoshi, Bijan 9
human rights 19–20, 22, 26, 28–30,
  37, 42, 43
human trafficking 24, 45, 73, 98,
  109–10, 129–30, 156, 177
  in Central and Eastern
    Europe 101–3
  and complex interactions 112
  complex systems of 68, 70, 91, 92,
    93, 109, 159
  congruity of goals between victims
    and perpetrators 131, 132, 144
  control over victims by
    perpetrators 82–6
  creating dependency 80–2, 120
  criminal justice framing of 37,
    41, 43
  criminal justice responses to 9–10,
    11, 157